Gentleman Trooper

How
John C. Groome
Shaped America's
First State Police Force

Harry G. Toland

EAGLE EDITIONS
2007

EAGLE EDITIONS
AN IMPRINT OF HERITAGE BOOKS, INC.

Books, CDs, and more—Worldwide

For our listing of thousands of titles see our website
at
www.HeritageBooks.com

Published 2007 by
HERITAGE BOOKS, INC.
Publishing Division
65 East Main Street
Westminster, Maryland 21157-5026

International Standard Book Number: 978-0-7884-4340-2

In memory of my mother,
Susan Groome Harney,
who was John Groome's
favorite niece.

Contents

v

Preface

A biographer of John Groome faces a handicap: an almost total lack of letters, journals, diaries and the like. So far as I can discover, a lone letter survives – in the Pennsylvania Historical Society's files. It is a completely perfunctory note from Groome, as House Committee chairman at the Philadelphia Club, granting permission for a man to use the club dining room for a party.

He did write a long article for *The Saturday Evening Post*, "The Riot Call," about his tour of duty as warden of Eastern State Penitentiary. He was quoted in occasional newspaper articles, but the *Post* piece is the only deep glimpse into his thinking. His descendants may exist, but I couldn't find them, even through newspaper ads.

The title of this book identifies Groome as a gentleman and a trooper. He was indeed a gentleman, not just in the standard understanding of the word in his day – a member of the "right" clubs and such trappings. He filled the role much more fully than that. He *believed* in gentlemanly conduct. When he briefed new troopers in the Pennsylvania State Police, for example, he told them, "It is possible for a man to be a gentleman as well as a policeman." Then he gave some particulars on how they could act like gentlemen.

He was a trooper first in Philadelphia's First City Troop and later as superintendent of the Pennsylvania State Police. Why are state policemen called "troopers"? I couldn't find anyone in the organization who knew for sure. My theory is that Groome, as the first superintendent, just liked the moniker and brought it over from the First City Troop.

From his years in the First City Troop and from studying European constabularies, he knew what worked and what didn't. He knew what principles would sustain such an organization. His touch was sure as he fashioned the Pennsylvania State Police.

"Groome made the constabulary famous all over the United States," said Governor Samuel W. Pennypacker, who appointed him. So famous, in fact, that a number of states modeled their police forces after Pennsylvania's.

His life cast him in other roles, too. He was a soldier, both in the National Guard and the regular Army, a much-decorated administrator of relief to starving survivors of World War I in Europe, and, as mentioned above, a prison warden. He won the admiration of Theodore Roosevelt and Herbert Hoover.

In a minor way he was a businessman as well. But it was his work with the State Police that gave him his niche in history.

. . . and Acknowledgements

A number of people helped in the preparation of this book and are remembered here with gratitude. Roxanne Carlson of Flintlock Press readied the manuscript for publication. Brenda Galloway-Wright at Urban Archives in Temple University's Paley Library dredged up numerous useful newspaper clippings and photographs. Dennis Boylan, the unofficial historian of the First City Troop, offered texts and background on the Troop. Erica Green, administrative assistant at Eastern State Penitentiary Historic Site, furnished copies of annual reports and other material. Jack Lewis, of the Pennsylvania State Police information office, delivered much usable material. Corporal Lucien Southard, of the Pennsylvania State Police, and Sergeant Kern Swoboda, of the New York State Police, supplied valuable photographs. Susan Gillis, archivist of the Boca Raton Historical Society, sent me helpful material. Clayton Platt, alumni director of the Episcopal Academy, made available school historical records. Shelley Leavens, director of development of the Pennsylvania State Police Historical Museum, provided pertinent insights into state police history. My sister-in-law, Mary Ann Wagner, enabled pictures to be taken of an important portrait.

And my wife, Sibby, and old friend and colleague Peter Binzen once again have read copy, found errors and offered valuable comments and support. To all, my sincere appreciation and thanks.

Harry G. Toland
Wallingford, Pennsylvania

1

Deployment

The 1910 transit strike in Philadelphia was the worst in the city's history and it evolved into a general strike, a historic first. In its sixty-two-day course twenty-nine people were killed either in clashes of police and rioters, of which there were four, or in accidents.

Hundreds were wounded or injured. About seven hundred of the newly electrified street cars were wrecked, many of them burned or dynamited by the 4,750 striking members of Division 477, Amalgamated Car Men's Union, or their sympathizers. Five thousand car windows were smashed. Property damage was put at $7 million, a staggering sum in those days.

The strike cost the Philadelphia Rapid Transit Company (P.R.T.) $1.5 million and all but bankrupted the private utility. The company imported 1,460 "new men"—scabs, in union parlance—from as far away as Omaha, Nebraska, to operate the cars, further inflaming the strikers.

The violence was completely beyond the control of the city's 3,300 police. Very early in the strike, which began on February 19, almost two hundred State Fencibles, a militia-like outfit, had been summoned to restore order. The crowds hung pretzels on their bayonets, ridiculed them and chased them off the streets.

Henry Clay, the city's director of public safety, asked Governor Edwin S. Stuart to send in the National Guard. Stuart demurred: that would cost too much and it was unnecessary, he said. He offered instead the State Police.

"When they have eaten up the State Police," he told Clay, "then I will give you the Guard." On February 23 Mayor John E. Rayburn asked the governor to make good his offer.

Late that afternoon Stuart's order reached the four State Police barracks—the most distant was in Greensburg near Pittsburgh—and was relayed to all their substations.

Some of the men had to ride their horses (the force was not yet motorized) sixty miles to join their troops. By midnight, men from all four troops (at Punxsutawney, Wyoming, near Wilkes-Barre, and Reading in addition to Greensburg) were entrained for Philadelphia. They arrived at 5 a.m., a mere twelve hours after receiving the order.

The response must have gratified their superintendent, Captain John C. Groome. The "staties" were the nation's first state police force, and from the beginning, in 1905, their leader had drilled into them the need for quick reaction to orders.

*

Clay and his police chief, John Taylor, had plans for deploying the 170 state troopers and their eight officers. They would be split up into small units and work under police captains in various parts of the city.

Groome flatly vetoed the plan. "I realized," he said later, "the danger that would lie in my men's working with city police under divided authority with no one really responsible for any mistakes that might occur."

"When they asked me what I would do," he continued, "I said that if they would give me a certain section of the city, not too large to be covered by 180 men, they could take all their men off the streets at 8 o'clock the next morning and I would be responsible for the maintenance of law and order in my section.

"I knew exactly what part of the city they would give me, Kensington, where they had had the most trouble—and they did." Specifically, an area of sixteen city blocks in that near-northeasterly section of Philadelphia.

Kensington was the city's biggest factory district with a dense collection of textile, clothing and hosiery plants, among others. Their workers were the car men's most loyal and passionate backers.

The troopers were lodged in one of the P.R.T.'s nineteen car barns, at 8th and Dauphin Streets, and their horses, which had been shipped in, were stabled there. The men slept on "shakedowns" of straw.

Early the following morning a double column of mounted troopers in their black uniforms and helmets—the Black Hussars, they were called—headed out on the one-mile trip to Kensington. Each trooper carried a holstered revolver and a pair of handcuffs but not their carbines.

Leading them, riding side-by-side, were Groome and his deputy, Captain George F. Lumb. The superintendent came from a patrician family of some wealth. He had been educated in a private school, was a member of Philadelphia's most exclusive clubs and a polo player of some note. He smoked imported cigarettes.

The background of Lumb, hand-picked by Groome as his deputy, couldn't have differed more sharply. Born into a poor family in London, England, he came to the United States via Canada, earned his living from age eleven, sold matches and soap on the streets, joined the army at age nineteen, winning promotion by personal bravery.

As the troopers reached Kensington, Katherine Mayo, who wrote the first history of the Pennsylvania State Police, *Justice to All*, described the action:

> "Without a word spoken, a command given or an eye turned, the crowd that had flocked out to curse and rail and stone fell back in silence, was absorbed into the alleys [and] houses, disappeared from sight.... Silently, the squadron moved through the Sunday streets...."

"Even the horses, filing past, drove their moral home. These were no sleek, fat, showy city mounts, but the small, wise, wiry, plainsman's breed, sharp and hard in long, thick winter coats that spoke the habit of rough, steady work in harsh and open country....

"As the squadron rode farther into the heart of the district, one of a rowdy crowd of sympathizers looking down from the windows of a tall factory flung a heavy steel bolt, striking a trooper in the back. The assailant instantly ducked out of sight, yet not quickly enough to escape the eye of the officer next to the man attacked.

"Vaulting out of his saddle, that officer made straight into the factory and, striding alone through its crowded halls, up several flights of stairs, reached the floor from which the bolt was thrown. With one glance at the mass of glowering humanity packed in the room, his practiced eye singled out his man.

"As unconscious apparently of every other creature present as if such did not exist, he gathered that one man into his grip, firmly propelling him through the throngs of his mates, down and out of the building and into permanent custody.

"A day before, the throwing of that bolt would have meant riot and bloodshed. Now, not a finger was raised, not a voice heard to resist the arrest."

*

Philadelphia—the entire nation, in fact—was seeing a new kind of police force in action: carefully trained, disciplined, determined to "get their man."

Groome divided his squadron into small units to cover the assigned district. Because the area was large and the number of men small, each trooper had to remain on duty eighteen hours. A number of arrests were made the first day, then order prevailed. In their entire deployment, not a single shot was fired by the troopers.

From that first day, streetcars were operated out of Kensington with no disturbance. Did that make the state police strike breakers? Close observers thought not. A Philadelphia magistrate, based on his personal experience in the strike, commented:

"No greater aid could have been brought to the strikers' cause. The general public, seeing no more bloodshed and riot, was led to infer that the labor people were now conducting their strike in a lawful and orderly manner. Public disfavor began to wane.... The cause of labor lost nothing but public antagonism by the advent of the State Police."

The troopers had visited Philadelphia earlier on a couple of ceremonial occasions. But, wrote the *Philadelphia North American*, "[This] first appearance here on any serious business awakened for them the respect and admiration of the whole town.... In the district which they patrolled all day there was not the slightest outbreak and by nightfall the State Police had inculcated a very friendly and wholesome respect among their observers."

From the *Pottsville Journal*, which had observed the Black Hussars up close in coal mine strikes, came this comment:

"We say with a degree of pride that no finer body of men ever sat a horse than the State Police of Pennsylvania.... When the State Police rode the streets of Philadelphia the people looked upon them not with hatred but with respect. Why? Simply because they recognized in them a force that stood for the law and only the law. Politics do not touch the State Police and neither does the power of the corporations..."

*

This was just how John Groome had trained his troopers to act and how he wanted them to be perceived by the public.

Later in the week, responding to an urgent appeal from authorities in South Bethlehem, Groome sent two of the troops there to quell violence in a steelworkers' strike. The remaining two troops stayed in Philadelphia and maintained order in their assigned area.

In the final eighteen days of the stoppage, the car men were joined by an estimated 146,000 workers in building trades and other industries, making it a general strike, believed to be a national first.

Settlement was finally reached on April 22 when Mayor Rayburn mediated an offer from the P.R.T. of minimum pay of two dollars a day for the car men. Philadelphia's worst strike was over.

2

"The Finest Thing in the World"

The first time John C. Groome was offered the job of superintendent of the Pennsylvania State Police, he turned it down. He had no experience in police work, he told Governor Samuel W. Pennypacker.

Technically, that was true. In reality, however, during his twenty-three years (up to 1905) with the First Troop, Philadelphia City Cavalry, a Pennsylvania National Guard unit, he had been involved in policing various disturbances and riots around the state.

He was captain of the troop in nine of those years. In each of the nine the First City Troop had received the U.S. Cavalry's highest rating for efficiency.

Pennypacker, who had been pondering his choices of superintendent for almost two months, knew all that. And he had promised legislators that this first chief would be a qualified man with no political connections. So he pressed his offer.

Groome was finally persuaded. But, mindful of Pennsylvania's notorious political spoils system, he issued a stern proviso: "If I take the task of organizing the new State Police," he said, "there will be no place in the force for political henchmen or ward politicians, no toleration of wire-pulling in any shape. If or when I cannot run it on this plane, I shall turn the commission back to the governor..."

This was no lip service. He followed up three years later with a general order:

"Any member of this Force known to have used outside influence for the furtherance of his interests will be considered as acknowledging his incompetence and will be dropped from the service."

Not long afterwards a lieutenant approached a state senator and a few other influential men asking their help in his quest for a captaincy. When their letters reached Groome, he promptly dismissed the lieutenant.

The governor, a former judge, was delighted by his new superintendent's stand. In his 1918 autobiography, Pennypacker wrote of Groome:

> He proved to be just the man needed, of the right age [43], slim, erect, quick to see and act, possessing a rare combination of decision, of character and sound judgment. I told him I wanted a police force and absolutely nothing else. Not a man on the force was selected on the recommendation of anybody.... Groome made the constabulary famous all over the United States.... They have maintained the peace within the state as was never done before. Not once has it been necessary to call out the National Guard, and that vast expense has been saved.
>
> While organized labor has unwisely assailed them as "Pennypacker's Cossacks," one of their greatest merits has been that they have saved labor from the oppression of force and have done away with the kind of police intervention, which came from men employed by the corporations (the Coal and Iron Police).

*

Much of the press also applauded, as in the *Harrisburg Telegraph*:

> It is fortunate that the experiment...is to be carried out under the supervision of an officer of the character and caliber of John C. Groome.... Into no better or safer hand could the work of organizing the force be

committed and his choice removes any misgivings as to the real aim of the new department.

The *Philadelphia Inquirer* followed with this point: "If Captain Groome will bring his State Constabulary up to the efficiency of the First City Troop, the State can hardly ask more of him."

Acclaim for the fledgling department was not universal, of course. At a meeting of three districts of the United Mine Workers in Shamokin, John Fahy, president of District 9, told his colleagues:

"The State Constabulary law—as is the Coal and Iron Police law—is an open insult to the working people of the State of Pennsylvania. I speak of the system, not the men comprising it. I don't know another state which legalizes men to do what these men can do."

The detailed 1905 act provided for a Harrisburg headquarters, (it was placed in the new state capitol) four troops, each with a captain, a lieutenant, five sergeants and fifty men, later identified in Groome's military style as privates. Location of the troops around the state was left up to the superintendent.

The salaries of all were specified, beginning with the superintendent's of $3,000 and his deputy's, $2,000. Privates got a meager $720, plus barracks accommodations and meals.

Groome's first deputy was a man with background much like his own, J. Cheston Morris. The son of a prominent physician and a graduate of the University of Pennsylvania, Morris was an executive of a Pottstown iron company and a fellow member with Groome of the Philadelphia Club.

He lasted only two years, however, resigning for health reasons. George Lumb who succeeded him was a veteran of years of army service in war and peace. The hero of a pitched battle with accused murderers that took the lives of two troopers, he had come up through the ranks in the State Police. He and Groome made an oddly assorted but effective team of leaders.

As Philip M. Conti wrote in his history, "The...suitability of this team remains unmatched in Pennsylvania State Police history."*

At the turn of the century when the Pennsylvania State Police was founded, America was in its Iron Age, or more specifically, its Steel Age, and Pennsylvania was its engine.

Great railroads like the Union Pacific were tearing up their iron rails to replace them with the stronger, smoother steel variety. The trains crossed rivers on bridges of steel. The skeletons of commercial buildings going up now were steel. Henry J. Heinz, launching his "57 varieties" in Pittsburgh, needed carloads of steel "tin cans."

The nation's thirty steel mills labored to meet the demands. Eighteen of the thirty were in Pittsburgh, Bethlehem, Johnstown and Steelton—powered by coke made from coal mined in southwest Pennsylvania's almost bottomless bituminous fields.

Fortunes were being made. In 1900 alone Andrew Carnegie's companies yielded $40 million in profits, of which the founder kept $25 million.

Hordes of European immigrants manned the mills sometimes clamorously, as in the Homestead strike and riot. Many of them lived in company towns, exploited by high rents and high prices in the company's stores.

When 100,000 textile workers shut down their industry in Philadelphia in 1903 to gain a fifty-five-hour work week, the strike failed but it brought to light a deplorable fact: ten thousand of the strikers were children, many of them only ten years old. Many years were to pass before effective legislation brought an end to the abuse of child labor.

---

* Conti, *The Pennsylvania State Police: A History of Service to the Commonwealth, 1905 to the Present.*

It was a time, too, of notorious corruption. Philadelphia earned its insult from Lincoln Steffens: Corrupt and contented...the worst governed city in the country.

In Philadelphia, with ten thousand city offices at the disposal of the Republican organization, each employee was told to kick back 3 to 10 percent of his salary. In 1903, the scheme netted the party $349,000.

In Pennsylvania the Matthew Quay machine skimmed millions from public contracts. Quay was replaced by the even more larcenous Boies Penrose, denounced by Theodore Roosevelt as a "force of evil."

The era wasn't all bad, though. Theodore Roosevelt, the trustbuster, was a strong force of reform, as were some who came after him like Pennsylvania's Gifford Pinchot. It was a time, too, of invention and ingenuity. Typewriters and phonographs took their place in the culture; motion pictures got their shaky start. In 1912 Leopold Stokowski took over the baton of the Philadelphia Orchestra with brilliant results.

*

In setting up the Force, "I proceeded very carefully," John Groome told Katherine Mayo, "There was no precedent, nothing to pattern by and the matter was as new to me as to everybody else."

One of his first acts was to hire John H. Clarke, of Langhorne, Bucks County, as the Force's chief clerk, plus a stenographer-typist. Clarke immediately began screening the one thousand applications that had flooded in.

Applicants had to be U.S. citizens between the ages of twenty-one and forty, and unmarried. They had to pass physical and civil service mental tests. A Philadelphia physician, Dr. Francis D. Patterson, traveled around the state giving examinations at fifteen locations.

Groome gave preference to men five feet six inches and taller and to those who had served in the army. Their final screening, including questions of conduct and morality, was by Groome himself. No other issues mattered.

The *York Dispatch* of that time quoted a Republican politician as asking Groome if he knew that "seven of your eight officers are Democrats." He replied, "I don't give a hoot whether the State Police Force is Protestant or Catholic, Republican or Democratic. I want men who can ride and fight."

The 193 men who survived all the screening became the original cadre of the Pennsylvania State Police. (Subsequently, they had to be brought up to full strength of 228.) They hailed from nineteen states and nine out of ten were army veterans.

To select locations of the four troops, Groome studied law enforcement needs around the state before choosing the sites near Greensburg, Punxsutawney and Reading and in Wyoming, outside Wilkes-Barre. Buildings were rented for barracks use. (The State Police did not have regular jurisdiction in cities with established police forces.)

"These sections," Mayo wrote, "by year-round criminal record, produced more murder, more manslaughter, more robbery, more rape, more burglary and theft, more lawlessness and disorder of every sort, by far, than [any] other parts of the Commonwealth."

The United Mine Workers laconically noted that the western two troops were in the bituminous field, the eastern ones, anthracite.

Groome had to bear in mind that his force also had responsibility for enforcing the law in the commonwealth's vast rural areas.

Finally, he wanted a model on which to pattern the new constabulary. He traveled to Canada, Ireland, England, Switzerland, France and Germany to study police forces. The model he chose was the Royal Irish Constabulary (RIC).

RIC features that he wove into the Pennsylvania fabric were: unmarried troopers living in military-style barracks available for instant duty, patrols fanning out from the barracks and a black uniform topped by a London-"Bobby"-type helmet.

There were significant differences, however: at the turn of the twentieth century the RIC had 12,100 police to cover 32,599 square miles with a population of 4.4 million; the Pennsylvania force of 228—one fiftieth of the Irish constabulary—was trying to deal with 6.3 million people living on 45,308 square miles.

Beyond that, the RIC, headquartered in Dublin Castle, was a British occupation force, loathed or at best tolerated by the people. Groome, by contrast, wanted Pennsylvanians to understand that this police force was working for them—was *theirs.*

*

Groome quickly put his stamp on the organization. Mayo quotes an unnamed trooper on the subject: "...above all the stiff training that each of us needed and got, ran the paramount influence of the superintendent's personality. It was that one man's mind, felt straight through the Force, that set the standard for us all.... It was and is a...call upon all the very best that a man can give."

After men were accepted into the State Police, Groome met with them individually or in small groups.

"Your duty," he told them with quiet emphasis, "is to make the Pennsylvania State Police Force the finest thing in the world." He gave them specific guidance:

"It is possible for a man to be a gentleman as well as a policeman."

"I expect you to treat elderly persons, women and children at all times with the greatest consideration."

"When once you start after a man *you must get him.*"

"In making an arrest you may use no force beyond the minimum necessary."

"One State Policeman should be able to handle one hundred foreigners."

If the last sounds like an ethnic comment, it should be remembered that this was an era when large numbers of Europeans had immigrated and joined work forces. Often they didn't speak English and knew nothing of American laws.

As to what else was expected of a lone trooper, this story, as told by Conti, has become legend in the Force.

The sheriff of Northumberland County called the State Police to report a riot in Mount Carmel and ask for assistance. The sheriff was told that the State Police would be sent to the riot scene immediately. He in turn notified the Mount Carmel authorities to expect help. When the mayor of the town met a lone mounted trooper approaching the community, he asked, "Where are the rest of the men?"

"I was given the assignment," replied the trooper. "There was only one riot reported."

Trooper training included much instruction by book and lectures in criminal laws, laws of evidence, game and forestry laws (one crime frequently encountered was the dynamiting of trout streams to collect fish).

Along with the instruction went daily drills, mounted and dismounted, the manual of arms and revolver practice.

They learned, too, the rudiments of detective work, something rarely seen in rural Pennsylvania. An example that Sherlock Holmes might have appreciated is recounted in the State Police annual report of 1908.

Private Herbert Smith and two other privates of Troop B, at Wyoming near Wilkes-Barre, were sent to investigate the theft of several hundred pounds of copper wire from the Moosic Lake Traction Company. They discovered that poles had been cut down for more than a mile and a large amount of copper wire stolen.

From marks in the road they found that a two-horse wagon had been used to haul the wire away. By following the wagon tracks, they found the stolen wire in the mountains nearby.

Smith noticed from the hoof prints that one of the two horses was shod with an oddly shaped bar shoe. "With this clue only," Smith and his colleagues followed the trail for *forty-three* miles to Carbondale, Lackawanna County. There they found the horse with the peculiar shoe in a livery stable.

"The three men who had hired the team were located and, being unable to account for their actions at the time the wire was stolen, were arrested. They have since been tried and found guilty."

The State Police had more serious matters to deal with, too. In the first seven years after they became operational on March 1, 1906, for example, they successfully prosecuted 102 murder cases.

Their most difficult crime problem in the early years were the predatory activities of the Black Hand Society, a forerunner of the Mafia. Black Hand members extorted money under threat of death or injury from Italian merchants, workers and others believed to have savings.

District attorneys asked the State Police to gather evidence against Black Hand members. "In 1907," wrote Conti, "the troopers undertook a campaign...to wipe out the influence of that society in the Commonwealth.

"Encouraged by the State Police and security from harm, victimized Italians and witnesses provided needed evidence. Arrests were made. District attorneys...successfully prosecuted in court. Severe punishment was administered by the courts. The work of the State Police in 1907 went a long way in wiping out the dreaded influence of the Black Hand in Pennsylvania."

Groome had to adapt his horse-mounted troopers to other challenges, notably the automobile and traffic control. This came to a head in July 1913 with celebration of the fiftieth anniversary of the Battle of Gettysburg.

Some fourteen thousand cars and wagons converged on the small Adams County town. Yet a Pennsylvania commission overseeing the event, observed that "so perfectly was the traffic being directed by the combined squadrons of the U.S. Cavalry under Major Rhodes and the State Police under Major Groome" that no accident of any kind occurred.

Earlier, in September 1906, he had had a more personal encounter with traffic control: Lower Marion police clocked him driving thirty-three miles an hour on Montgomery Avenue in Ardmore. Two patrolmen testified he had covered a marked course of 825 yards in fifty-two seconds.

"I never run under ten miles an hour," Groome told a justice of the peace. "The machine won't do it. So I suppose I must have been going too fast." The newspaper headline called it "A Great Burst of Speed." He was fined fifteen dollars and costs of $3.83.

*

The mundane but necessary work of equipping the troopers began with their horses. Groome signed on a Philadelphia veterinarian, Dr. C. J. Marshal, to purchase horses, all of them in Texas.

Marshal made two trips to the Savage and Conover Ranch to buy 230 horses at $115 each. They were relatively small—most of them under fifteen hands (five feet)—meeting U.S. Cavalry standards, light feeders and bred for endurance. They were shipped directly to the four troop headquarters where stables had been prepared.

Each trooper was issued a .38 caliber Colt revolver, a twenty-two-inch hickory baton, a pair of steel handcuffs and a .45 caliber Springfield carbine, to be used only in special emergencies.

Their uniforms, similar to the RIC's consisted of a military tunic and riding breeches of charcoal gray whipcord, black boots, pigskin puttees, buckskin gauntlets and the reinforced helmet.

A distinctive feature, required by Groome, was a 7/8-inch nickel letter showing the policeman's troop, and his personal identification number. Both were riveted on either side of his tunic collar.

They could not be removed without destroying the garment. Their purpose was to allow a complainant to readily identify a trooper.

*

None of the constabulary's good work cut any ice with its most implacable enemy, James H. Maurer. Born in Reading, Berks County in 1864, he was a newsboy at age six and a factory worker at ten. In 1906 he was the Socialist Party candidate for governor. He became president of the Pennsylvania Federation of Labor and was first elected to the state House of Representatives in 1910.

"At last," he said after that election, "I shall have an opportunity to strike a blow at the Cossacks, Pennsylvania's murderous, legalized band of strike breakers."

Maurer was barely seated in the House before he introduced a bill to repeal the act that established the State Police. It was sent to the Judiciary Committee where it died.

The battle continued over another bill, also in the spring of 1911, to increase the pay of state troopers. Maurer led the opposition. Groome wrote to the House in behalf of the legislation:

> ...a great deal [has been said] about the State Police Force being used to the injury and detriment of the working classes. This all has its origin in a few professional organizers whose very livelihood depends upon disagreements between capital and labor...there are records in the office which show that the majority of intelligent working men are in favor of the Department of State Police for the following reasons:
> Previous to the creation of this Force, whenever labor disturbances occurred, it was the custom of sheriffs of the counties to swear in great numbers of

deputies who were recruited from the ranks of the unemployed in the cities without [investigating] their character, morals or fitness for...duties of a police officer. These men were armed with Winchester rifles or revolvers. They were undisciplined and as a rule drank excessively.

It is impossible to think that a man of average intelligence would prefer to have such characters doing police duty...in preference to trained men who have to produce bona fide proofs of their excellent character, pass a rigid physical and mental examination and who are responsible to bonded officers of the Commonwealth for their actions....

The bill was passed by both houses of the legislature and sent to the governor who signed it. It was the troopers' first pay increase and affected all ranks, from the deputy superintendent whose salary was raised by $500 to $2,500, to privates who went from $720 to $900. All but the superintendent whose pay remained unchanged.

This was a signal victory for Groome and his men, even though he had tried and failed to win an increase in the size of the force. Three years earlier he had vainly asked the legislature to add two troops, enact a pension for troopers and benefits for widows and men injured in the line of duty.

Passage of the pay increase did nothing to deter Maurer, however. In 1915 he wrote a booklet published by the Pennsylvania Federation of Labor titled *The American Cossack*.

In it he called the State Police, "a new labor crushing device" who come in contact with workers "only when called upon to beat and kill them.... Let us get rid of them that Pennsylvania may return to the old-time peaceful condition."

Groome set out to refute his charges one by one. No worker had been illegally killed in any of the troopers' riot-control encounters, he said. Maurer charged that State Police beat and killed workers in the 1910 Philadelphia transit strike. Groome responded that not a shot had been fired by his men in that strike.

As for "the old-time peaceful condition," said the superintendent, that included the Molly Maguire reign of terror in the 1870s and the later Homestead and Lattimer riots.

He summed up: "No honest, law-abiding citizen, no matter what his occupation or station in life, has any reason to fear or to oppose the State Police, as Maurer very well knows."

Maurer must have known he was fighting a losing battle. Six years earlier when Groome decided that a worsening crime problem in Schuylkill County merited moving C Troop barracks there from Reading he met a storm of protest.

Reading, Maurer's hometown, sent delegation after delegation to beg Groome not to remove the troop. The *Reading Times* wrote, "...the members of this troop have won and held the admiration and confidence of the law-abiding citizens of the entire section of the state."

So much for the "murderous Cossacks" of Maurer's diatribe.

*

Groome and his Black Hussars finally won vindication in 1917 legislation that increased the size of the force along with another pay rise.

Both were desperately needed. More than 37 percent of the troopers had left in 1916 for higher paying positions elsewhere, Groome told Governor Martin Brumbaugh.

A key indicator of acceptance in the House was the votes of Luzerne County legislators. In 1913 and 1915 they had voted down similar increases. But they had been impressed by the peacekeeping work of the State Police in the 1916 transit strike in Wilkes-Barre.

In 1917 five of the eight legislators switched and voted for the increases. This despite legitimate criticism during debate on the bill that Groome spent most of his time in Philadelphia where he lived, leaving day-to-day operations to his deputy, Lumb, in Harrisburg.

The system seemed to work, however. "Groome was an excellent administrator," wrote Conti, "and handled his liaison duties with governors and legislators tactfully. He was an appealing personality, waxed mustache and all."

In 1916, when the entire force was tied down with problems in the eastern part of the state, trouble erupted in the west. Groome was urged to detach troopers for duty in the west. Here is Mayo's account of his reaction:

> "I cannot do it," said he. "It would be deserting the field. It would be giving criminal encouragement. It would be subversive of public morale."
>
> "Then," he was told, "you must add to your force to meet this emergency."
>
> "How?"
>
> "Why, hire more men, of course."
>
> Said the superintendent of State Police:
>
> "Given the best of material and the hardest of work, it takes over a year to make a State Police officer.
>
> "Do you think I would trust that uniform to a stranger, with the chance of his disgracing it? If you wanted a larger State Police, the time to think of it was in the last Legislature. Now you must abide by your decision."

The 1917 bill for the first time increased the size of the force—by 102 men to 330, or 44 percent. Privates' pay went up from $900 to $1,020. And Groome's salary, which was not increased in 1911, was doubled from $3,000 to $6,000.

It was as solid an endorsement as one could ask for.

3

Origin

What would prompt a normally conservative state like Pennsylvania to create something that no other state in the Union had—a state police force?

Clearly, it would take an event of seismic proportions. That earth-shaking occurrence arrived in the form of the Anthracite Coal Strike of 1902, which lasted more than five months (from May 12 to October 23).

Close to 150,000 miners in 357 collieries, demanding better pay and shorter hours, quit work. The flow of anthracite, the hard, high-carbon fuel of choice in millions of homes, schools, businesses, etc.—the legendary "black diamonds"—dwindled to a trickle. Its price, normally five dollars to six dollars a ton, tripled. A rise in pneumonia death rates was attributed to the fuel shortage. The Eastern seaboard was particularly affected but the emergency was national.

The strike spawned violence, frequently caused by the infamous Coal and Iron Police, some 4,500 men hired off the streets by the companies but commissioned at one dollar apiece by the Commonwealth. The mine and railroad owners said twenty men were killed; the United Mine Workers put the number at seven.

To try to restore order, Pennsylvania Governor William A. Stone ordered out, first, units of the state's National Guard, then in the strike's final weeks the whole 8,750-man division, to keep order. That included Philadelphia's First City Troop, led by its captain, John Groome.

The deployment cost the taxpayers $996,000, a compelling factor in the later creation of the Pennsylvania State Police.

The walkout was historic, not only because of the number of strikers and its massive impact, but because it prompted the first presidential intervention in a labor dispute. The energetic, activist Theodore Roosevelt brought the parties together, then named a commission, ultimately settling the dispute.

The cast of characters was stellar, beginning with T.R. and his brilliant Secretary of War, Elihu Root. It included J. Pierpont Morgan, the financier and wire-puller who had a moderating influence on management in the dispute; George F. Baer, the operators' truculent leader and John Mitchell, the conservative, statesmanlike president of the United Mine Workers, who ended up capturing the public's sympathy.

*

The miners' grievances were all too real. They put in ten hours a day of hard and dangerous work. Frequent layoffs brought their average pay down to about three hundred dollars a year, less than six dollars a week. Miners' children had to work in the pits, Mitchell said, to bring family income up to a living wage.

Accidents killed 441 miners in 1901, and mine owners did nothing to enhance safety or compensate workers for injuries.

The strike that began on May 12 was labeled temporary by the UMW. The union then called a convention in Hazleton to determine whether the walkout would be made "permanent."

Mitchell counseled against a long-duration strike. "Is it better," he asked the delegates, "to go on improving your conditions little by little or to risk everything in one great fight?" The roll call vote on making the "suspension permanent," however, was 461¼ votes in favor and 349¾ opposed.

Mitchell observed later that "the instructions of the delegates [from the men they represented] made it impossible for them to defer to my judgment." After the vote, the delegates reportedly cheered him until they were hoarse, and their leader shed tears.

Mitchell, who started working in the mines when he was twelve, became head of the UMW in 1898 when he was only twenty-eight. Foster Rhea Dulles in his *Labor in America* attributed Mitchell's rise to his skill in organizing the many nationalities working in the mines:

"Slight and wiry, with brown eyes and a swarthy face...he had a modest almost diffident manner. His strength was in his patience, his conciliatory attitude both in union politics and in employer relations and his willingness to compromise on anything but what he thought were major issues."

"No labor leader of the period," said Dulles, "was more conservative in his social and political attitudes, more willing to accept arbitration or more disapproving of radicalism and violence...."

Some in the union urged Mitchell to call out the miners in the bituminous field to support the strike. The UMW leader refused. "They have a contract that must be honored," he said.

As the strike wore on, the public and the press increasingly came to support Mitchell and his union over the intransigent operators.

George Baer, president of the Reading Company, a coal-carrying railroad, adamantly opposed recognition of the union and the arbitration that Mitchell offered. His aim was to "break the strike." His most memorable act was to write what became known as "the divine-right letter."

A Wilkes-Barre man named William Clark had written to Baer appealing to him on Christian grounds to settle the strike and asking God to "send the Holy Spirit to reason in your heart and to act accordingly...."

Baer responded: "...you are evidently biased in favor of the right of the working man to control a business in which he has no other interest than to secure fair wages for the work he does. I beg you not to be discouraged.

"The rights and interests of the laboring man will be protected and cared for—not by the labor agitators, but by the Christian men to whom God in His infinite wisdom has given the control of the property interests of the country...."

Public derision punctuated by hoots of laughter followed. The Hearst papers blasted Baer for "crass and horrible...blasphemy." The *New York Times* commented, "A good many people think they superintend the earth, but not many have the egregious vanity to describe themselves as its managing directors."

*

As the strike dragged on and cold weather approached, Roosevelt was under intense pressure to get the dispute settled and coal moving through the pipeline again.

His first effort was to call together in the White House on October 3 Mitchell and district leaders of the UMW and heads of the coal and railroad companies. The conference was a dismal failure.

The union, Mitchell said, was willing to accept the findings of any commission the President appointed. Baer again flatly rejected any arbitration, verbally attacked the miners and scolded the President for seeking to negotiate with "the fomenters of...anarchy and insolent defiance of the law."

Roosevelt was reported to have exploded later, "If it wasn't for the high office I hold, I would have taken him by the seat of the breeches and the nape of the neck and chucked him out of that window."

In a letter that evening to Ohio Senator Mark Hanna, T.R. wrote, "None of them appeared to such advantage as Mitchell whom most of them denounced with such violence and rancor that I felt he did very well to keep his temper. Between times they insulted me for not preserving order..."

An immediate result of the White House conference was Governor Stone's calling out the entire Pennsylvania National

Guard. The move was in response to the operators' claim that if adequate protection were provided, the miners would return to work.

Mitchell and the union's district chiefs called meetings of the strikers to declare that the management statements were false. They voted unanimously to continue the strike, Mitchell told the president, and emphatically denied that fear of bodily harm was keeping them away from work. Roosevelt himself observed that the deployment of the whole Guard brought only "a trifling increase" in the number of men working.

Other stratagems were floated and shot down. A desperate Roosevelt then hatched a radical plan: send in the U.S. Army to take over the mines, and notify the miners to resume work. Under the plan, Governor Stone would notify the president that he could not maintain order and ask for help.

Because it was so drastic—and probably unconstitutional—Roosevelt told only one person about his idea, retired General John M. Schofield whom he had picked to lead the takeover. But word reached Elihu Root.

Alarmed about the possible consequences of the army deployment, Root offered the president an alternative: appoint a commission which would hold hearings and make binding recommendations; meanwhile, the miners would return to work.

Roosevelt told the secretary to go ahead and try to get both sides to agree to his proposal but that he was acting on his own, not on the president's behalf.

Root first set up a meeting with J. P. Morgan. They talked on the financier's yacht *Corsair*, anchored off the West 35th Street pier in New York. "With Morgan's approval," wrote Robert J. Cornell, "Root then drafted an arbitration offer.... It was prepared for the coal operators to sign and issue as emanating from them, offering to submit the points at issue to a commission to be appointed by the president...." The UMW was given no status in the deal.*

Morgan apparently did not have much trouble convincing the operators to go along with the Root proposal; most of them by then were feeling heavy public pressure to get the strike settled before cold weather set in.

Baer, the pit bull of the negotiations, appeared to fade into the background as Morgan quietly wielded influence. Mitchell told an interviewer: "I am credibly informed that he is friendly to organized labor."

Morgan's key role in the settlement was acknowledged by Roosevelt, who later wrote to him:

"And now, my dear sir, let me thank you for the service you have rendered the whole people. If it had not been for your going into this matter I do not see how the strike could have been settled at this time.... I thank you and congratulate you with all my heart."

*

But the makeup of the commission that would do the arbitrating became a thorny issue. The management people specified that they wanted a five-man commission, identified by occupation or title and tilted toward their interests.

Mitchell objected strongly, and Roosevelt went to work to deal with his complaint. He got agreement on adding to the commission a sixth member, a bishop from Peoria, Illinois, who he thought would favor the union.

He wanted a union leader on the panel but the operators rejected the idea. One of the five members, however, was listed as "a man of prominence, eminent as a sociologist."

The president saw a possible way out of the impasse. Suppose he named E. E. Clark, grand chief of the Order of Railway Conductors, as the "eminent sociologist"? He floated

---

* Cornell, *The Anthracite Coal Strike of 1902.*

this transparent fraud before Robert Bacon and George Perkins, Morgan aides who had come down from New York to press for a settlement.

"To my intense relief," Roosevelt wrote a few days later, "this utter absurdity was received with delight by Bacon and Perkins, who said they were sure the operators would agree to it."

That broke the deadlock. The commission now had two members leaning toward the operators, two toward the miners and two who were impartial—acceptable to both sides.

With Mitchell's assurances, the mine workers met in convention, accepted the presidential commission plan and agreed to return to work on October 23. Roosevelt immediately called on the commission to start meetings the next day.

The commission began hearings on November 14 and issued its full report on March 21, 1903, its terms to be in effect for three years. It awarded the miners a ten percent pay increase and, for most workers, a cut in daily work hours from ten to nine.

In what amounted to de facto recognition of the UMW, the panel called for establishment of a board of conciliation to settle grievances, with three miners' representatives, three for the operators and a court-appointed umpire to break tie votes.

On the question of keeping order during the strike, the commission came down hard on the Coal and Iron Police:

"The employment of this body of police is authorized by law, but they are really the employees of the coal companies and thus do not secure the respect and obedience to which officers of the law are entitled. Their presence is an irritant, and many disturbances in the coal regions during the late strike grew out of their presence."

They proposed a pioneering alternative: "Should this matter be remedied by legislation, so that the laws could be enforced and peace preserved by a regularly constituted constabulary, appointed and paid by the county or state, the Commission believes that much of the disorder which accompanies strikes would be avoided."

Governor Pennypacker needed no convincing. He was by nature and record something of a reformer; he played a leading role in civil service reform in Pennsylvania.

Born in Phoenixville in 1843, at twenty he enlisted as a private in a Union regiment and fought at Gettysburg. He "read the law" in a lawyer's office, attended something called the Law Academy and was admitted to the bar. In 1889 he became a judge in Philadelphia's Common Pleas Court.

When he was nominated for a second ten-year term, he was lauded by the *Evening Bulletin* as "clear-headed, industrious, wise and faithful [in] performance of duty." He was later elected presiding judge of the court.

When he was nominated as governor in 1902, President Theodore Roosevelt said his defeat would be "a national calamity." He was elected easily and sworn in the following January.

Throughout his political career, however, he remained close to Pennsylvania's two most renowned spoils-system politicians, Quay and Penrose.

Early in his term as governor, he let it be known that if the (highly political) state Republican convention was to nominate him for a seat on the state supreme court, he would accept and run for election. This was picked up by the press, generating something of a scandal.

Forty-three Philadelphia lawyers—the cream of the bar—wrote him saying that if he went to the supreme court in that manner he would "forfeit a large share of the respect and esteem of the profession and weaken the faith of the people in the disinterested administration of justice."

They added, "We do...earnestly entreat you to reconsider your avowed intention and to continue to the expiration of your term as governor...."

In his autobiography, Pennypacker wrote: "Nothing that occurred during my whole term gave me as much pain as this communication." He dropped the idea and served out the remainder of his term as governor.

*

It was too late in 1903 to introduce legislation establishing a constabulary. And since the legislature met every other year, the matter had to wait until 1905.

In his message to the lawmakers that year, Pennypacker declared, "The State stands above interests in controversy and its powers ought not to be used by either of them." He proposed appointment by him of a constabulary of sufficient force, say ten in each county [670], to be used wherever needed in the state in the suppression of disorder.

He followed the message with bills in both houses of the legislature. The one in the Senate, with minor amending, sailed through on a 40-0 vote. The House was another story.

One assemblyman called Pennypacker's proposal a joke, estimated that it would cost the state $500,000 (he was close) and told his colleagues, "Let us kill it now."

Others picked up on the cost issue. Organized labor was fearful that a state police force might be used as a private army against them. The end result whittled down the proposed force from 670 to 228. Finally, some wanted to know what political patronage would accompany the new force.

When all the concerns were answered, the House passed its bill 156-28. The law the governor signed on May 2, 1905, left little to the imagination.

It called for an appropriation of $425,000, spelled out the number of troops (four), the personnel and salaries of officers and men, their powers (like those of police in first-class cities). The State Police, the act stated, "are intended, as far as possible, to take the place of the police now appointed at the request of the various corporations." The Coal and Iron Police were thus officially doomed.

All that was needed then to start the Pennsylvania State Police on its way was the governor's call to John Charles Groome.

4

Katherine

In August 1913 Katherine Mayo, then forty-six, was visiting a lifelong friend, Moyca Newell, at her country estate in Bedford Hills, New York. A construction crew was working on the grounds.

Early one Saturday morning a young foreman of the crew named Samuel Howell was headed toward the site on his motorcycle. He was carrying the week's payroll. Less than a mile from his destination four men armed with revolvers ambushed him. They demanded the payroll.

Without hesitation, Howell drove his cycle through the gang who pumped seven bullets into his body at close range. Mortally wounded, he managed to drive to the work scene, deliver the payroll and positively identify two of his attackers. Then he collapsed. Three days later he died.

His assailants, former laborers at the project, spent the rest of the day lying low in a clump of woods not far from the crime scene.

Katherine Mayo spent the day gathering facts about the shooting. The county sheriff and some village constables who showed up "proved utterly unrelated to the emergency," she said. "I saw the complete breakdown of the sheriff-constable system."

Talking with the construction boss, she asked, somewhat naively, why his men didn't surround the murderers in the woods.

"We earn our living on country jobs among men like these," he told her, motioning to the unskilled laborers gathered around him. "Knives and guns are their playthings, and when they want me they'll get me, just as they got poor Howell.

"We have to think of our families. We can't afford to earn the gunmen's ill will. There's no protection in the country districts. Sheriffs and constables don't help us at all."

Then he added words that burned into Mayo's mind: "Howell was only a working man. You'll have forgotten him in a month."

His prediction couldn't have been more wrong. The attractive, wealthy, idealistic Mayo never forgot, in fact used the case as the starting point for a law-and-order crusade with national implications.

Over and over she questioned: how could effective law enforcement be brought to rural sections of the state? Perhaps because she had been born in Pennsylvania (Ridgeway) and had connections there, she had heard of the Pennsylvania State Police, then it its eighth year.

A police force like that, she reasoned, would have been able to go after Howell's murderers.

"I therefore went to Pennsylvania to study the facts at first hand," she wrote in the foreword to "Justice to All." "This book is an attempt to bring the facts nearer to public reach."

The book, a compendium of facts and impressions, was the first to tell the story of Pennsylvania's constabulary in any detail. Its frontispiece photograph is of John C. Groome.

*

In a stroke of genius Mayo lined up Theodore Roosevelt to write the book's introduction—Roosevelt, not only a former president and governor but former head of the New York City Police Commissioners.

"...the State Police of Pennsylvania, under its superintendent, Major John C. Groome, has furnished a model which is to be studied everywhere..." he wrote.

"The Pennsylvania State Police is a model of efficiency, a model of honesty, a model of absolute freedom from political contamination."

In some places with frontier conditions, like Texas and Arizona, he said, ranger outfits have partially met the need for rural policing.

"But there is no other body so emphatically efficient for modern needs," he added, "as the Pennsylvania State Police. I have seen them at work. I know personally numbers of the men in the ranks. I know some of the officers."

And then this ringing endorsement: "I feel so strongly about them that the mere fact that a man is honorably discharged from this Force would make me at once, and without hesitation, employ him for any purpose needing courage, prowess, good judgment, and entire trustworthiness."

In 1915, the year before he penned the introduction, he wrote, the Force's conviction rate for arrests made was 80 percent—"the men are so trained and schooled in the criminal laws of the State that they know just what evidence is necessary."

Just as Katherine Mayo would have wished, he concluded: "The sooner all our other states adopt similar systems, the better it will be for the cause of law and order and for the upright administration of the laws in the interests of justice throughout the Union."

Roosevelt personally saw to it that every legislator in New York received a copy of the book as they pondered legislation to create a state police force. They passed the bill in 1917.

The Mayo book was considered a powerful factor in the enactment which made New York—twelve years after Pennsylvania's pioneering step—the nation's second state to field a police force.

The organizers of New York's constabulary pressed Groome to come and head it, but he rejected their plea.

The state police concept quickly gathered momentum. By 1922 the list of states with such forces also included

Massachusetts, Connecticut, New Jersey, Maryland, West Virginia, Colorado and Michigan.

Those in New York, New Jersey, Massachusetts and North Carolina specifically modeled their organization after Pennsylvania's, according to Shelley Leavens, development director of the Pennsylvania State Police Museum.

To some extent, then, Groome could claim paternity of the national state police force movement.

*

In her later years, her hair gone snow-white, Mayo continued to live on the luxurious Newell estate.

She developed a friendship with Lynn G. Adams, Groome's successor as superintendent of the Pennsylvania State Police. She and the Adams family visited back and forth in each other's homes.

In her full-length dresses and with her British upper-class accent, she was a memorable personage. She neither smoked nor drank.

"Miss Mayo traveled in style," Conti recounted, "with a luxury station wagon driven by a uniformed French chauffeur. For stays in New York, she maintained a Park Avenue apartment."

When Katherine Mayo died in 1940 at age seventy-two, the New York State Police honored her by assigning twenty-five troopers to act as pallbearers at her funeral. She was buried at Bedford Hills, the scene of the Howell murder.

"She was truly a great woman," wrote Conti, "and law enforcement in general owes her a debt of gratitude for the influence she brought to bear..." in New York state and elsewhere.

*

Katherine Mayo could hardly have foreseen today's Pennsylvania State Police. With a total personnel of 4,338, it is nineteen times the size of the original force, making it one of the five largest state constabularies in America.

The all-male, all-white force of John Groome's time has changed over the years, as could be expected. The first African-American was admitted in 1954 and the first woman in 1972.

Now, African-American troopers number 259, other racial minorities 41 and women 181. Instead of four troops, the force is now divided into sixteen.

An important part of the troopers' work is still criminal investigation, but that is now bolstered by wiretapping, forensic services and extensive records. As in all of its duties, the force's jurisdiction covers the whole state but troopers try not to overlap with local police.

Traffic patrolling and speed control are another major assignment as anyone who has seen a trooper in a Smoky Bear hat in his rearview mirror can testify.

Enforcement of liquor and drug control laws are other major parts of the force's work. Its members also are on call to deal with bomb and aviation emergencies. A SWAT team and a K-9 unit are now parts of the organization.

But diligent police work in solving crime problems— questioning crime victims and suspects and piecing together the puzzle—is still a staple of State Police procedure.

That is what led them, in early 2006, to arrest two young men from Herminie near Pittsburgh in a string of nineteen burglaries in Westmoreland County.

A bizarre aspect of the break-ins, to which the suspects confessed, was that they used the stolen goods as barter for things they wanted.

Just before the opening of antlered deer season, for example, one of the pair wanted a rifle for hunting. So they stole an all-terrain vehicle and worked out a deal with a friend to exchange it for a .30-caliber deer rifle.

At last report, they were being held in the Westmoreland County Jail under a $25,000 bond.

5

John Charles

It is unlikely that any other police chief in the nation belonged to the likes of the Philadelphia Club, the Racquet Club, the Philadelphia Country Club, the Philadelphia Cricket Club, the Merion Cricket Club, the Radnor Hunt Club, the Philadelphia Polo Club and The Rabbit, a gentlemen's eating society.

But John Groome, a joiner if ever there was one, was a member of all these exclusive bodies at one time or another.

The public didn't seem to notice. People, first, were deeply grateful that he wasn't a political hack and, second, they came to be highly impressed with the way he set up and ran the State Police. So his personal life, which generated no scandals, was ignored.

Some of the club memberships were extensions of his sporting interests. He played cricket and polo; he shot pigeons, hunted quail and the fox and played tennis and golf.

His favorite was polo because, he said, "it requires teamwork and strategy, good horsemanship and nerve, and a good physique"—attributes he had in full measure.

He was good at polo, a member of the team that played the first polo game in Philadelphia and captain of the First City Troop polo team, which defeated teams of the Sixth U.S. Cavalry in Washington in 1896. The Troop team gave their opponents a handicap of five goals and still won by a score of 7 to 5 ¾.

This was the first match ever played by officers against a team not in U.S. service and marked the beginning of recognized polo in the regular army.

John Groome played the game for fifteen years and was a member of the National Polo Association's executive committee.

The only part of his private life that drew occasional comment was that he lived at home. This was in stark contrast to the troopers' mandatory barracks life—to be ready for instant duty—and the location of the constabulary's headquarters in Harrisburg.

When he visited Harrisburg, he stayed at the Lumb home, an arrangement apparently acceptable to the Lumbs. Otherwise, he could keep in touch by a relatively newfangled service, the telephone.

Groome's homes were gracious and at good addresses— then and now. He lived at 1018 Clinton Street in Philadelphia, a three-and-a-half story brick row house in a tree-lined block just west of Pennsylvania Hospital. It is now broken up into apartments.

Later in life he acquired a "country home" at Railroad Avenue and Polo Road in the Main Line suburbs between Bryn Mawr and Haverford. The privet border of its yard gave the large three-story house its name, "Green Hedges."

Just across Railroad Avenue at Polo Road was a polo field where Groome probably played. A baseball diamond and a lacrosse layout now take up the space. "Green Hedges" has been replaced by a large nursing home.

He shared homes with his wife, Agnes Price Roberts, of Philadelphia, a handsome woman whom he married on April 15, 1884. The couple had three children: John, Jr. (who also became captain of the First City Troop), Agnes and Martha.

A member of the Society of Mayflower Descendants and the Daughters of the American Revolution, Agnes Groome had a pedigree to match her husband's. During World War I she was vice chairwoman of Emergency Aid of Pennsylvania, which collected funds and clothing for servicemen.

*

John Charles Groome was born in Philadelphia on March 20, 1862, one of six children of Samuel W. Groome and his wife, born Nancy Andrews Connelly.

The Groomes descended from Captain Samuel Groome, a mariner from Middlesex, England, who settled in Kent County, Maryland, about 1650. Around 1770 another ancestor, Charles Groome, built a house he called Hopeful Unity, a brick structure of 840 square feet plus kitchen wing. It still stands near Chester, Maryland.

John was probably named for John Charles Groome, another forebear who was an early nineteenth century general.

The former's father, Samuel, had a weakness for the bottle, which led to financial straits and doomed John's hopes of attending the University of Pennsylvania.

Like King Lear, Samuel late in life took to visiting several of his children, each for months at a time. The routine in those stays was to supply Groome pere with a glass of whiskey before each meal, including breakfast. Booze may have contributed to a breakdown of communications between him and Nancy; they spoke only through a servant.

The family home was at 1914 Spruce Street, a four-story brick row house with a ten-foot paneled wood front door. It, too, has been converted into apartments. It was and is an excellent address.

John's education began with private tutors at home and was completed at the Academy of the Protestant Episcopal Church, one of the best private schools in the city.

The school, now The Episcopal Academy, occupied a large, bleak-looking three-story stone building at Locust and Juniper Streets, a seven-block walk from the Groome home. The academy's course of studies at the time was anything but "gut."

It included English elocution and grammar, arithmetic, algebra, geometry, natural science, ancient and modern geography, Latin grammar, Cicero, Horace, Greek grammar,

Homer's Iliad, Xenophon's Anabasis, French, history, sacred studies and Bible history.

John did not receive a scholarship commendation from the school in his final year, as did some of his classmates, but that may have had something to do with his young age. He graduated in 1878 at sixteen.

*

He was considered a handsome young man by his contemporaries, his dark hair parted in the middle and a mustache with waxed tips.

He joined his father in the iron commission business, but didn't like it. He and his brother, Harry, bought a small stock farm in Wythe County, Virginia, and operated it for several years.

When he returned to Philadelphia he went to work for Hutchinson & Company, wine merchants and importers. Having learned the business there, he formed his own company, Groome & Co., in 1902.

During debate in the state House in 1913 over increasing the size of the state police, John's reputation as a businessman was attacked. Rep. Daniel J. Shern (R-Philadelphia) rose to his defense:

"Mr. Groome conducts a wholesale liquor business at the corner of Camac and Walnut Streets," he said, "but he only sells to his intimate friends—and three or four clubs—the highest grades of champagne...and wines. And I know whereof I speak, that he has not a saloon upon his books. Superintendent Groome is highly respected in the community."

He was not active in the business and considered himself a sort of silent partner. Today his dual role as police chief and head of a business would probably be considered a conflict of interest.

In 1914 he helped form a brokerage firm, Goddard, Groome and Drayton Company, and served as its vice president until 1920 when his tenure as head of the state police expired. Then he joined George W. Kendrick and Company, an investment banking and brokerage concern.

The Groomes were members of historic St. Peter's Episcopal Church at Third and Pine Streets, Philadelphia. At least, that's where John and Agnes were married and out of which he was buried. How often they attended is not known.

*

John Groome must have had a way with horses, somewhat as General Ulysses S. Grant did. For starters, he was a slim five feet nine, giving him a good riding and racing weight. But his horse connection went far beyond riding. The First City Troop Annals spell out details and in the process sketch a picture of public transportation—even commuting—at the time:

> Captain Groome was a well-known whip and devoted much time to coaching.... In the spring of 1892 he and Barclay H. Warburton drove the public road coach "Meadowbrook" daily from Philadelphia to Willow Grove and return.
>
> In the summer of 1893 he drove the road coach "Alert" for two months daily from the Hollywood Hotel in Long Branch, N.J. to the Monmouth County race track and return.
>
> He was one of six Philadelphians who drove the public road coaches "Vivid" and "Alert" between Philadelphia and New York daily during the spring months of 1894. One coach departed Philadelphia for New York and one left New York for Philadelphia each day at 8 a.m. and arrived at their destinations at 8 p.m.
>
> Seventeen four-horse teams were used each day, and the distance, ninety-two miles, was covered in

twelve hours, including thirty minutes for lunch in Princeton.

During the following spring Captain Groome drove the road coach "Champion" daily from the Stanton Hotel, Philadelphia, to the Philadelphia Horse Show at Wissahickon Heights and return, and later in the season drove the "Alert" from the Stanton Hotel to Meadowbrook Farms and return....

This was no easy job. The whip had to steer and control four horses with which he may have had little or no familiarity and control the coach itself when that became necessary. The presumption is that he was well paid for his services.

He won prizes for driving four-in-hand teams in horse shows in New York, Chicago and Philadelphia. He was in demand also to judge at horse shows, which he did in those cities and twice at London's Olympia.

None of this could have been considered training for the superintendency of the State Police, but it clearly built a bulwark of self-confidence in the man.

6

The City's Troop

John Groome joined the First Troop Philadelphia City Cavalry (First City Troop) in 1882 just shy of his twentieth birthday.

In the twenty-eight years he served in and led the Troop before going on the honorary roll in 1910, he learned the basics of leadership, command presence and discipline that he took with him into the State Police and elsewhere.

Some might see the Troop as a surprising school for leadership training. It was as much a gentleman's club as a military unit. The public knew the troopers mostly for ceremonial turnouts in their toy-soldier full-dress uniforms.

Yet when they were given gritty assignments by the Pennsylvania National Guard in peacetime or war they tackled them with the zeal and discipline that would have credited a veteran regular army outfit.

The First City Troop is special in many ways. It was founded on November 17, 1774 by twenty-eight "gentlemen of fortune," to use George Washington's phrase, and served with him in the battles of Trenton and Princeton.

"...they have shown a noble Example of discipline and subordination, and in several Actions have shown a Spirit of Bravery which will ever do Honor to them and will ever be gratefully remembered by me," the Commander-in-Chief wrote to the Troop's captain, Samuel Morris.

The Troop is the oldest continuously serving mounted unit in the U.S. military.

Unlike the rest of Pennsylvania National Guard where a volunteer signs on by enlisting, First City Troop volunteers must be elected—in Groome's time and today. Officers also are elected in the Troop although they must be militarily qualified.

After being appointed corporal and sergeant, John Groome was elected first lieutenant in 1894 and captain two years later. Endorsing his leadership, the Troop twice re-elected him; his fourteen-year captaincy was the second longest in Troop history at the time he left active service.

*

The ceremonials began early. In 1885 John and his brother, Harry, both privates, were among twenty-seven troopers on hired horses making up the only cavalry unit in the parade at President Grover Cleveland's inauguration in Washington. They were in full-dress uniform.

Resembling those of royal horse guards at Buckingham Palace, the uniforms included a busbee helmet with a bearskin topper, fringed epaulets on a tunic with strands of silver braid stretched button-to-button across the chest, piping on the sleeves, a baldric (ammo) box on the back held by a cross-chest sash, white leather gauntlets, skin-tight white riding breeches and black leather Wellington boots with spurs. Hanging by the mounted trooper's side was the scabbard for the saber he held and an ornate dispatch case.

In Groome's captaincy the Troop, so garbed, turned out eight times to escort visiting presidents. The most memorable of these was the appearance of Theodore Roosevelt in 1905 to highlight University Day exercises in the Academy of Music.

Afterward, they invited the President back to the armory on 23rd Street at Ranstead for lunch, the first president since Washington whom the Troop had entertained at a meal. Groome toasted the president who responded:

"There is no other voluntary organization in the country…that has [a] standard 130 years old, a standard that foreshadowed our present national flag, no other organization that has the letter of Washington thanking it for its services in the Revolutionary War, no other organization which has served…on each and every occasion when the country's welfare, menaced by foreign or domestic enemy, required its services."

They then tied into grapefruit, strained gumbo with amontillado, diamond-back terrapin, squab chicken, romaine salad and Camembert.

Ceremonial occasions sometimes took the troopers far afield. In 1904 two officers and thirty-eight men traveled to the St. Louis Exposition to escort Governor Pennypacker on the expo's Pennsylvania Day. They spent three days taking in the exhibits before heading home.

The Liberty Bell went nowhere without a Troop send-off. In 1895, when the bell was taken to the Atlanta exhibition, forty troopers in full-dress uniform, led by Groome, marked its departure.

Eight years later when the bell was requested in Boston at an anniversary of the Battle of Bunker Hill, troopers accompanied it to the railroad station.

*

But the gritty assignments couldn't wait. The most important in Groome's captaincy was the Spanish-American War, which began April 5, 1898.

On April 28 the captain and fifty-nine troopers, joined by ten more later, entrained for camp at Mt. Gretna. They were armed with carbines, sabers and revolvers. Groome, as senior officer, was given command of the three cavalry troops at the camp.

For ten weeks they took two long marches each day plus drills and target practice with the carbines and revolvers. The troop was ordered to come to one-hundred-man strength. In late July they moved on to a camp in Virginia and four days later were ordered to Puerto Rico.

Boarding the troop transport *Massachusetts* were Groome and two other officers, a surgeon, ninety-eight enlisted men, 104 horses and twenty mules.

The passage to the island was not a Caribbean cruise. The ship was painfully overcrowded with barely enough water to keep men and stock alive.

Then, following a dispatch boat toward the harbor of Guanica on the southern coast, the ship ran aground on a coral reef. After vain efforts to float it free, lighters were needed to take the men and horses off the ship.

On August 12 Groome received orders to move the troop to Guayama, fifty miles to the east near the southern coastline. Two miles north of Guayama on the road to Cayey was an artillery battery in position to fire on Spanish "entrenchments."

Groome's orders were to have his troopers dismount, unsaddle horses and await the artillery's attack in advance of their own. Troop annals pick up the story:

"At 11 o'clock, just as the battery had received the order to commence firing, [Major] General [John R.] Brooke received by mounted messenger from Major General [Nelson A.] Miles an order to suspend all military operations, as a peace protocol had been signed by the United States and the Spanish government."

The cavalry troops returned to Guayama. For almost two weeks men and horses went to the beach for daily swims. Then on August 25 they were ordered to Ponce, some thirty miles to the west on the southern coast.

The Troop made camp just south of the city along the Rio Portugues. But the river, swollen by rainy-season downpours, overflowed its banks and flooded the campsite.

The troopers ended up in Playa de Ponce, a seaside suburb, according to the Troop annals, sitting on curbstones "in heavy rain, each man holding his horse by the bridle reins"—as forlorn a military scene as could be imagined.

They embarked for New York on September 3 on the troopship *Mississippi* for a voyage with privations much like the one that took them to Puerto Rico.

Back in Philadelphia, at the request of Mayor Charles Warwick, the Troop paraded through streets lined with cheering people and were guests of the city at a dinner in Horticultural Hall.

The Troop annals sum up the five-month deployment: "Under canvas at Mt. Gretna and Newport News, in shelter tents at a dozen different camps in Puerto Rico during the rainy season, and spent twelve days going out and coming home on overcrowded, unsanitary transports.... Every man was always ready for any duty, and there was not a single case of serious illness in the entire command."

It is something of a Troop tradition to bestow silverware to commemorate notable occasions. Thus, a year later, relatives of the Puerto Rico volunteers gave the Troop a silver punch bowl two feet in diameter with an ebony base carrying silver plaques bearing the volunteers' names.

Yet a question arises: if an engagement like Puerto Rico was memorialized by a silver punch bowl, what would have been given after, say, the Battle of the Bulge or Iwo Jima?

*

Some of the Troop's difficult assignments were previews of actions Groome would oversee when he became superintendent of the state police. A prime example was the famous Homestead riots of 1892.

John Groome and his brother, Harry, both sergeants at the time, were among fifty-two Troop members dispatched to Homestead near Pittsburgh when the whole Pennsylvania National Guard was called out by Governor Edwin Stuart.

A disagreement over wages between workers and management at the Carnegie Steel plant in Homestead led to the workers taking over the plant and the town. When the company tried to bring three hundred watchmen into the plant, gunfire was exchanged and several men on both sides were killed. The mob burned the barges which had brought the watchmen.

The Troop spent two weeks patrolling and suppressing violence. Brigadier General Robert P. Dechert, the cavalry brigade commander, said of their work: "They are entitled to great credit for the arduous duties...of that campaign."

The strike helped Grover Cleveland win re-election later that year and the strikers' defeat retarded unionization of steelworkers for more than forty years.

The first of such deployments after Groome had become Troop captain was an anthracite coal miners' uprising in Luzerne County in 1897.

The disturbance reached a climax in a confrontation of the workers and a sheriff and his deputies who killed more than a dozen miners and critically wounded many others.

The next day at 11:30 a.m. Groome received orders from Major General George Snowden of the Pennsylvania National Guard to bring the Troop to Hazleton. In four hours the members, in service uniforms and armed with carbines and sabers, entrained at the Baltimore and Ohio Railroad station at 24th and Chestnuts Streets.

They arrived at Hazleton at 9:30 p.m., ten hours after receiving the order. The speed of their response was evidence of Groome's taut-ship style.

From September 12 to 28 they made daily mounted patrols of fifteen to twenty miles to surrounding towns. When they were relieved on September 28, the Pennsylvania National Guard thanked the Troop for "the efficient manner in which they have discharged every duty assigned them."

In an assignment whose appropriateness he couldn't have guessed at the time, Groome and his troop were dispatched to restore order in the great anthracite coal strike of 1902, which resulted in the creation of the Pennsylvania State Police.

The troopers—three officers and fifty-four enlisted men—were sent to Tamaqua in Schuylkill County. For the next four weeks they made two-day patrols and occasional night forays within a fifteen-mile radius.

Having endured heat in Puerto Rico, they now experienced the other end of the thermometer—temperatures below twenty degrees most of the time. On November 7 they were transferred to Hazleton with daily patrols continuing. With the strike settled, they returned to Philadelphia on November 12.

Service in difficult engagements continues in modern times. Troopers served in Bosnia and, as of 2005, nine members were on duty in Iraq, said Dennis Boylan, a former captain and the Troop's informal historian.

Money seems not to have been a problem for the troopers. When a former captain, Edward Grubb, got married in London in 1891, for example, John Groome, his best man, and five other troopers as ushers booked ocean liner passages to stand by their friend.

Then and now the members turn over their National Guard paychecks to the Troop to meet its expenses. No other Pennsylvania National Guard unit does that. In Groome's day most of the members were socialites; today, much less so, Boylan said.

The Troop has always had a connection with the Episcopal Church. One of the three events it has long observed each year is the death of George Washington on December 14.

On the Sunday closest to that date, uniformed troopers used to turn out at St. James Episcopal Church at 22nd and Walnut Streets. After that church was torn down in 1947, the observance was moved to either Christ Church at Second and Market or St. Peter's at Third and Pine, both Episcopal parishes.

The other dates the Troop marks are its November 17 birthday, when the organization's elections are held, and Washington's Birthday on February 22.

Nuts-and-bolts issues also had to be dealt with in the Groome captaincy. A forty-eight-hour snowstorm in 1899 collapsed the roof of the riding hall of the armory on 21st Street near Market.

The building had to be abandoned. The Troop bought the lot on 23rd Street and put up a replacement, occupied in 1901 and still in use today. It also houses the Troop museum.

*

John Groome, known to some of his colleagues as "Groomie," was held in their affection. In Troop tradition, they used silver to express it.

In 1907, to mark his twenty-five years of service in the Troop, he was given a silver loving cup. Private Henry S. Drinker, lead partner of Drinker, Biddle and Reath, one of the city's most prestigious law firms, presented the cup.

Three years later, on November 17, when Groome resigned as captain to go on the honorary roll, the troopers gave him a six-piece silver tea service "as token of their regard and esteem."

With it went an engrossed letter expressing the members' regret at the resignation of Captain Groome, "a man, a soldier and a companion."

He responded, passing on his feelings on receiving "this mark of friendship and esteem of the Troop and my own deep regard for the Troop which was so near my heart during the most active years of my life."

John C. Groome as first superintendent of the Pennsylvania State Police. (*Pennsylvania State Police photo*)

John C. Groome as captain of the First City Troop, Philadelphia.
(*First City Troop photo*)

In full-dress City Troop uniform. (Oil painting by Carl Ludwig Becker [1820-1900], Groome Family Collection)

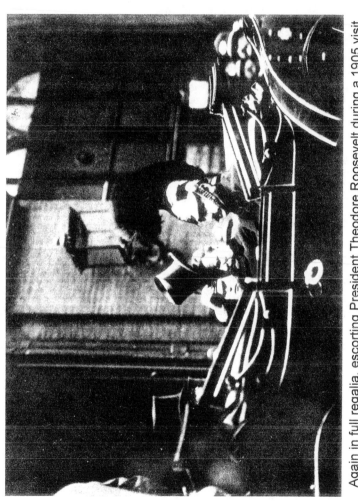

Again in full regalia, escorting President Theodore Roosevelt during a 1905 visit to Philadelphia. (*First City Troop photo*)

Groome's home at 1018 Clinton St., Philadelphia, Pennsylvania.
(Photo by author)

Agnes Groome in a 1924 photo.
(*Urban Archives, Temple University, Philadelphia*)

Portrait of John C. Groome hanging in the Racquet Club,
Philadelphia, of which he was a member. (*Courtesy the Racquet
Club, Philadelphia, artist unknown*)

Detail of a portrait of Katherine Mayo, first historian of the
Pennsylvania State Police. (*New York State Police photo*)

Eastern State Penitentiary, its cellblocks spreading out from the octagonal hub.
(Photo: Andrew J. Simcox, 1997. Courtesy of Eastern State Penitentiary Historic Site,
Philadelphia)

John C. Groome in 1924 when he was warden of Eastern State Penitentiary and under grand jury attack. A later investigation cleared him of charges. (*Urban Archives, Temple University, Philadelphia*)

7

War, Struggle and Relief

was a foregone conclusion that John Groome would become
volved in World War I, but no one could have guessed the
ried and extraordinary duties that service would bring him.

One of those assignments—perhaps his finest hour—was
anaging the distribution of food after the war in the three
altic states and part of Russia amid extreme turmoil. The
fort saved tens of thousands of lives.

World War I began in the summer of 1914, but the United
ates didn't enter the conflict until April 6, 1917, in protest to
erman submarine attacks on shipping.

The American Expeditionary Force (AEF), commanded by
eneral John J. Pershing, landed in France in June 1917,
hered in by Pershing's famous salute, "Lafayette, we are
re."

John Groome, fifty-five at the time, heard the call. While
maining state police superintendent (Lumb became acting
per) he offered his services to the army on October 20 of
at year.

The army's response was mystifying. This veteran
valryman and career police chief they made head of military
telligence in the air service of the Signal Corps. He was
mmissioned a lieutenant colonel and stationed in
ashington.

Assuming, apparently, that military intelligence included
lice work, Groome began recruiting experienced detectives,
cluding four officers of the Pennsylvania State Police.

He sailed for France February 1, 1918. When he arrived he
as appointed inspector on the staff of the chief of the AEF's
r service.

At some point the AEF must have waked up to Groome's background. In May, Pershing transferred him to the Provost Marshal General's office and by July he had been made acting Provost Marshal General, a job he filled for four months.

That made some sense. The Provost Marshal governed the military police, did criminal investigations and was responsible for prisoners of war and traffic control.

Groome made a detailed study of British military police methods and with that information made recommendations for a reorganization of the American MPs.

He sent a lieutenant on his staff back to the States to recruit 150 qualified men for special MP duty. He was looking for men forty to fifty years old, preferably with business or executive backgrounds, men of tact and judgment.

Their role, he said, would be to establish friendly relationships with Allied civil and military authorities and solve problems. With no mention of further training, they would be given commissions as first lieutenants, captains and majors.

Groome later set up a more standard military police training school in Autun, 150 miles southeast of Paris.

His prisoner-of-war duties put him in charge of forty thousand prisoners captured by American forces. He supervised the building and operation of the Central Prisoner of War Enclosure at Tours, 125 miles southwest of Paris.

At one time the camp, which became quite famous, held ten thousand prisoners of war. British and French authorities called it a model facility.

*

In September 1918 Groome was promoted to colonel in the Signal Corps. Two months later the Armistice ended the war. Then came an entirely unexpected but enjoyable assignment.

During the war, leaves had been severely restricted. With the war ended, the Army rushed to make up for lost time. The AEF set up a Leave Areas Bureau and put Groome in charge.

"We hope to give them a chance to play," he told a Philadelphia *Public Ledger* reporter who came to Tours to interview him. "We are arranging for 50,000 at a time on eight days' leave.

"We are selecting the famous scenic and cure resorts of France and are trying to plan it so that all the men can be given a vacation before they go back to the States."

Quartermaster Corps officers were dispatched to twenty leave areas in France to confer with principal hotel keepers and get contracts signed.

The agreements provided for sleeping accommodations and meals in some detail. Dinner, for instance was to include "soup, roast with vegetables or 'pates', pudding or dessert, bread, tea or coffee with sugar and milk if possible."

The "amusement of the troops" was contracted out to the YMCA which Groome said was doing a "splendid" job. "They usually obtain a casino," he added, "and we send up a military band...[the men] will be given every opportunity for rest and recreation compatible with good discipline."

Officers' leaves were handled by a separate bureau, also headed by the colonel. Altogether, 75,000 officers were lodged in 120 Paris hotels, including the old Hotel au Lonore—newly named the American Officers' Hotel—which could accommodate 525 at a time.

Groome figured that the leave program, at no cost to the personnel, saved the officers a total of $750,000. He gave no estimate for the enlisted men.

*

His stint of relief work, as hectic as it was humanitarian, began early in May 1919 with an exchange of letters between

Herbert Hoover, head of the American Relief Administration (ARA) and General Pershing.

Two years earlier President Woodrow Wilson had called on Hoover to assemble a team to feed and clothe the hungry and starving in a score of post-war European nations, with special emphasis on saving children. The Hoover team consisted of 2,500 Army and Navy officers.

"Our operations in the Baltics are so intimately connected with the British," Hoover wrote to Pershing, "that in selecting the chief of the mission, I have been particularly careful to select a man who can tactfully handle this relationship.

"Colonel John C. Groome appeared to be the best man available...." He asked Pershing's help in expediting the transfer, which the general agreed to.

What made the food distribution difficult and at times impossible was the political and military strife going on in the Baltic states between German, Communist and local forces.

With the Armistice, each of the Baltic nations had established provisional democratic governments. Hoover described the situation:

"The Germans had created an army of occupation mostly of Balts [German-oriented Baltic 'barons'] and White Russians under German officers with General [Rudiger] von der Goltz in command.

"...with the [Reds] spreading Communism by infection and by attacking armies, with the Balt element endeavoring to control the governments, with an uncontrolled German-commanded army in their midst, and rank starvation everywhere, these people were fighting on four fronts."

In the midst of this turmoil, John Groome with thirty-six officers and a cadre of enlisted men was trying to distribute food to the starving.

The contingent, which included also clerks, mechanics and interpreters, left England on a United States destroyer assigned to Groome's use and arrived at Libau, Latvia, on May 31, 1919.

Parallel to American relief operations in all three nations
ere similar but much smaller British units with whom
roome had to coordinate his work.

*

That there were starving people was beyond doubt. Here is
ie scene on the docks of Riga, the capital of Latvia and
rgest city in the Baltics, as sketched by Lt. Col. A. J. Carlson
f the Groome contingent:

"Scores of children and old people lined up on the quay
efore the American food ship *Lake Mary* and the British
estroyer *Vancouver* in mute appeal for food. They fought for
arbage from the ships' kitchens. With old tin cans tied to
icks they picked up the garbage that was thrown overboard,
ven to raw potato peelings.

"Children and old women begged for the privilege of
weeping the quay where American food was being
nloaded.... With their bare hands or with a rag they would
weep the stones for the little flour that dusted through the
ick, then pick out the larger particles of dust or dirt [and put
iem] in a handkerchief or directly into their mouths...."

The sight had emotional impact on John Groome. "It makes
ie sick to go on the streets and see these kids," he said.

In Estonia, the smallest and most northerly of the states,
iey mortality rate of children from starvation in some towns
ie previous year had been as high as 35 percent, according to
.oover.

Early in 1919, the relief workers scrounged flour cargoes
om Finland, Denmark and England. Regular food shipments
arted coming into the country when Groome and his group
rived, allowing for a program of free feeding of children to
e started.

From that feeding program, Hoover wrote, "a lasting
npression has remained in the Estonian mind."

All told, Groome and his cohorts distributed 53,554 tons of food and 4,179 tons of clothing and medical supplies to Estonians, at a cost of $18.6 million to the United States.

All the while an Estonian peasant army reinforced by Finns, Swedes and White Russian volunteers was battling Communist fighters from Russia.

The situation was far worse in Latvia, the middle state. A council of Letts had set up a republic at Riga, led by Karlis Ulmanis, a key figure in the independence movement in all three Baltic states.

The Balts opposed his newly hatched government with the result that he was unable to overcome a Communist uprising early in 1919 supported by a Red army invasion from Russia.

"We were about to land food supplies," wrote Hoover in his memoir, "when Ulmanis and his government were forced to retreat underground."

In the spring, however, he was able to establish headquarters for his government at Libau on the coast and he renewed appeals to the ARA to fight starvation.

The relief organization ordered a cargo into Libau, wrote Hoover, and "in a week they had kitchens operating and were feeding some twenty thousand of the most distressed people."

A week later the Balts, led by large land owners and "surreptitiously supported by von der Goltz's army, seized Libau." Ulmanis had to flee again, this time to Sweden, bringing a halt to ARA food distribution.

On April 20 a squadron of Allied destroyers appeared off the Latvian coast causing von der Goltz to back down. Food distribution then resumed.

As if this on-and-off rollercoaster ride wasn't enough, a general breakdown in law and order followed in Riga with an even more desperate need for food. Hoover sent a telegram to von der Goltz (whose duty under the Armistice was to keep order in the Baltics) asking him to occupy Riga.

As soon as he agreed, Hoover told his people to deliver food to the city immediately. Just days before Groome arrived, forty railcars loaded with foodstuffs from Libau headed out for Riga.

The last ten miles of railroad tracks, they discovered, had been destroyed. Much of the food, therefore, had to be transported by wagons and even handcarts before the tracks could be re-laid. By late May, Lt. George P. Harrington and his men were providing one meal a day to 200,000 people.

Meanwhile, the communists had set up a makeshift government which had opened the prisons and turned the inmates loose on the public. Here is Hoover's account:

"Together with the communists they looted every store and house.... Literally hundreds of innocent people were daily executed without trials in a sadistic orgy of blood.... The deaths from starvation and other causes were so many that coffins could not be provided and bodies by the hundreds were dumped into trenches."

Soon, however, von der Goltz and his army ousted the communists and set up a military court dominated by Balts to try those guilty in the Red purge. A White scourge now replaced the Red terror, prompting American protests.

Hoover, admitting that he had no particular authority in the matter, sent a telegram to John Groome:

"...The Germans are responsible for this white terror which succeeded the red terror in this instance.... As soon as you get to Reval [now Tallinn, capital of Estonia], see the various military commanders, communicate to them my views and secure from them a definite assurance that the Riga incidents were not to be repeated. Tell them plainly that you are directed by me to see that these unlawful and inhumane acts do not occur....

"The American people will not lend their support for an instant to any movement which would countenance such actions. Show this telegram to Admiral Cowan and General Gough." It was signed "Hoover."

The Germans then began limiting their executions mostly to proved criminals. Ulmanis returned to Riga and set up a provisional government, supported by food shipments organized by Groome.

But more fighting broke out, this time between the Letts (native Latvians) and the Balts. Again, John Groome was called into the fray.

"Colonel Groome and Lieutenant Harrington took a distinguished part," wrote Hoover, "in making an armistice and bringing various elements together into a temporary coalition under Ulmanis against the communists."

After that, Hoover noted, the relief administration set up a free feeding program for fifty thousand "stunted children" and another for adults. "It performed a healing service not only to bodies but to spirits," the ARA chief wrote.

"On June 28, the day the peace was signed in Versailles," wrote Hoover, "citizens of Riga, Libau and other towns came, with their children, in parades of thousands to the offices of our organization bearing flowers, with bands playing 'Yankee Doodle,'—their view of our national anthem—but they brought also tears and prayers of thanksgiving."

It must have been a moving moment for John Groome and his crew.

Altogether, the American feeding effort cost close to $7.5 million in Latvia and dispensed 41,200,000 "meals served to undernourished children."

Lithuania also had been torn by German and communist armies battling across its land. But the ARA managed a general relief program and child feeding which restored forty-five thousand children to health, according to Hoover's records.

Before the Americans pulled out of the Baltics they arranged for shipment of several thousand tons of seed grains to all three nations. It arrived in time for spring planting.

*

The final phase of the ARA's relief work was in northwest Russia which borders on Estonia and Latvia. Petrograd (now St. Petersburg) is only eighty-five miles from Estonia.

In the spring of 1919, a conglomerate army of White Russians, Finns, Estonians and Letts, commanded by General Nicholas Yudenich, proposed to capture Petrograd from the communists.

The Reds had come to power in the Russian Revolution a year and a half earlier, but in 1919 the country was torn by a civil war between the communists and what was left of the czarist regime.

The State Department asked Hoover to distribute food to people liberated in the path of Yudenich's army and to be prepared to feed the Petrograd population. One hundred thousand people were dying of hunger each month in the city, according to "authentic" reports Hoover had received.

Yudenich's army finally advanced over an area with 400,000 residents. A Captain Miller on Groome's staff reported on what they found:

"The communists on their retreat had plundered the district of what little food and livestock the people had, and machine-gunned the resisting peasants."

Yudenich got within a few miles of Petrograd when his army fell apart, looting some of the ARA storehouses in their retreat.

"Nevertheless," wrote Hoover, "we had fed some 400,000 starving people and left them enough food to get through until the next harvest.

"The affair dallied along until early July when I directed Colonel Groome to use elsewhere the stocks we had built up in preparation for the fall of Petrograd."

Altogether, Groome had supervised the distribution of foodstuffs and a small amount of clothing and medical supplies from the United States worth $31.9 million.

It was a part of an extraordinary life-saving American enterprise that saw to the donation of 19.3 million tons of food and goods in twenty-two European nations.

Hoover summed it up this way: "...this operation saved the Allies millions of human lives; it saved the peace-making; it saved large parts of Europe from Communism; it saved millions from starvation and restored at least 15,000,000 children to health."

The Marshall Plan following World War II is often cited as a foremost example of America at its generous best. The work of Hoover, Groome and thousands of others, while different, surely equaled the spirit and aim of the post-World War II effort.

Maxim Gorky, the Russian writer, wrote to Hoover: "In all of human suffering I know of no accomplishment which in terms of magnitude and generosity can be compared to the relief that you have actually accomplished."

*

His work with the Hoover mission brought Groome a shower of impressive decorations. England's King George V dubbed him a companion of both the Order of the Bath and of the "Most Distinguished Order of St. Michael and St. George."

French Premier Georges Clemenceau made him an officer of the Ordre de l'Etoile Noir (Order of the Black Star). The White Russians conferred on him a hereditary knighthood of the Order of St. Vladimir. And Estonia gave him the Croix de la Libertie.

Finally, two years after he returned to his native land, the Army pinned on him a Distinguished Service Medal with two clasps for "exceptionally meritorious performance of a duty of great responsibility." It is the Army's highest non-combat decoration.

8

Eastern Pen

In the last major chapter of John Groome's multifaceted career the became warden of the famous—or infamous—Eastern State Penitentiary, then one of the world's best-known prisons.

The job would present him, at age sixty-one, with perhaps the sternest challenge of his life. It would win him less renown than his leadership of the State Police did, and it would bring down public criticism on his head. But he would clean out the mess at the Pen and, with official commendation ringing in his ears, leave it a far better prison.

With his work completed in France and the Baltics, he sailed for home on October 5, 1919, and arrived in New York ten days later. Ten days after that he got his honorable discharge from the Army and was commissioned a colonel in the reserve corps cavalry.

Before that, of course, came the reunion with Agnes and their kids and the resumption of home life on Clinton Street. He took some well-deserved time off in November before reporting back to the State Police in December.

George Lumb was glad to welcome him back; having become a lawyer through nighttime studies, he was eager to practice law in Harrisburg. With Groome on the scene, he handed in his resignation as acting superintendent.

Groome appointed Captain Lynn Adams deputy superintendent. The following March, Adams began a record seventeen-year tenure as superintendent.

Then, looking forward to retirement himself, Groome turned to a couple of constabulary matters.

It had become ludicrously clear that troopers mounted on horses could do nothing more in policing speeding motorists than eat their dust.

In 1920, therefore, he inaugurated motorcycle patrols, each cycle attached to a sidecar. On the basis of early experience, the superintendent said they were "modestly effective in curtailing accidents, carelessness and speeding."

He also moved the constabulary's training center to Newville in Cumberland County, taking over the old Big Spring Hotel and its ten acres of land.

Then, effective February 28, he handed his resignation to Governor William C. Sproul, ending fifteen years of service to the Commonwealth. If there was a retirement ceremony for the first superintendent, it is nowhere recorded.

Back in private life, he severed connections with Goddard, Groome and Drayton Co. and joined George W. Kendrick & Co., bankers and brokers, also of Philadelphia, presumably of brighter financial prospects.

*

In 1923 the board of trustees of Eastern State Penitentiary urgently sought the services of John Groome. The board's president, Alfred W. Fleisher, twice offered him the warden's position. Twice he rejected the bid.

He had served the commonwealth in several capacities; he was making money with the Kendrick firm. "I did not want it and do not want it now," he told an *Evening Bulletin* reporter.

But the prison was in drastic straits. Five weeks of riots had rocked the institution, brought on by poor food, corrupt and low-paid guards, lack of sufficient work, overcrowding and dirt.

What sparked the riots was the oppression imposed by "The Four Horsemen," a gang of convicts assigned by penitentiary authorities to root out a thriving drug traffic.

"The appointment formed the basis of an authority," Groome wrote in his long *Saturday Evening Post* article, "which the four amplified and used for nearly every other purpose than the one intended..."

Those purposes included selling jobs, sex and favors and led to formation of a rival, warring gang. Many inmates were pleading to be locked in their cells to escape the conflict's violence.

That problem was ultimately solved by transferring one of the "horsemen" to Western State Penitentiary and the other three to county prisons. But that was only the first lap.

A grand jury early in 1923 saw "prisoners so drunk they could hardly stand." The jurors bought heroin from one inmate and real beer (Prohibition was then in force) from another. Two women in the female prisoners' cellblock had conceived and borne children in Eastern. The grand jury's report led to the firing of Warden Robert J. McKenty.

These were some of the conditions that brought Fleisher to Groome's doorstep a third time. The trustees desperately needed a firm hand at the prison, as well as a man of "humanitarian impulses." They knew of his reputation with the State Police and probably had heard of the prisoner-of-war camp he set up and operated in France.

John Groome finally capitulated, but not until he had conferred with Governor Gifford Pinchot.

The governor, he wrote, "looked a bit dubious at my demand for an absolutely free hand as a condition of acceptance. Though he recognized it as an emergency situation, he feared that I might 'introduce military discipline' into the penitentiary, and appeared startled when I admitted that this was exactly what I should do—at once."

Groome explained to Pinchot "the essential difference between a disciplinarian and a martinet, and mentioned the rigid military discipline as the basis on which I had organized the State Police," he wrote.

The governor at length gave him the green light and Groome accepted the appointment. "I am taking it at great personal inconvenience, but since the prison inspectors [the trustees' earlier title] believe that my services may be of help," he told the *Evening Bulletin* reporter, "I am willing to do my best."

*

When Groome took over Eastern State Penitentiary in June 1923, it had a century of history behind it.

ESP was the successor to the notorious Walnut Street Jail in which male and female prisoners were confined in a large room together. The strongest ruled, sexual dalliance was common and for a time the warden sold liquor to inmates from his own bar.

The new prison, built on a green rise of land called Cherry Hill north of what was then the city, was a reaction to the tumultuous Walnut Street institution.

Eastern State was founded on the Quaker principle that a prison, far more than punishing an inmate, should bring him or her to penitence for their crime (thus, "penitentiary"). For this, they were thought to need solitude and meditation.

The principle guided the physical plan, rules and governance at Cherry Hill. It was carried out to fearsome lengths.

From an octagonal hub, seven spokes radiated out, each cellblock with two courses of cells, all the corridors visible from the hub. The whole is surrounded by a thirty-foot stone wall. When it opened in 1829, it was the largest and most expensive structure in the young country.

In the beginning, each eight-by-twelve-foot cell, with its own small outdoor exercise yard, housed one inmate. Prisoners were fed in their cells and were forbidden to communicate with each other, verbally or by tapping messages. The only person the convict saw—occasionally—

was his overseer. Each cell had a flush toilet and central heat, services the White House had yet to acquire.

If the inmate had to leave his cell, say, for a religious service, he was required to wear a hooded mask over his head to avoid being recognized by fellow convicts.

Charles Dickens, visiting Cherry Hill in 1842, was appalled. "There is a depth of terrible endurance," he wrote, "in which none but the sufferers themselves can fathom and which no man has a right to inflict upon his fellow creature."

"I am persuaded," he added, "that those who devised this system of Prison Discipline and those benevolent gentlemen who carry it into execution do not know what it is that they are doing.... I hold this slow and daily tampering with the mysteries of the brain to be immeasurably worse than any torture of the body...."

The great writer had put his finger on the crux of Eastern State's problem. In the phrase of *The Times* of London, the system was "maniac-making." Although not to prison doctors, who held that any mental illness at Cherry Hill was caused by masturbation.

At the same time, it should be noted that prisons then were notorious dumping grounds for the mentally unstable.

Cherry Hill's physical form and system, nonetheless, became the model for some three hundred prisons around the world, from England, Italy and Russia to Japan and China.

Bit by bit, reality eroded ESP's separation system. By the turn of the twentieth century, the prison held 1,400 prisoners, twice the number it was built for, with up to four in a cell, all communicating. And wardens, conceding the obvious benefits, allowed outdoor team sports to be played.

*

By the time he began his wardenship, Groome had moved from Clinton Street to "Green Hedges" in Haverford. By the book, he was supposed to live in the warden's residence on the prison grounds, described in the *Evening Bulletin* as "grim and gloomy," with high, barred windows and stone walls that "reek of penitentiary atmosphere."

Having an "absolutely free hand," he spurned the residence regulation and commuted daily by car from the Main Line.

In the *Saturday Evening Post* article he told of his first visit to the prison. On a June night shortly after his election, he arrived at Cherry Hill at 11 p.m. in his chauffeur-driven car. The first thing to strike him was the "stench" of the Pen.

The second "was the sight of two or three hundred prisoners wandering around the corridors calling on friends...and hailing guards with familiarity by their first names.

" 'Who are these?' I asked.

" 'Trusties,' said one of the guards. They were nearly all elderly men, these guards.

" 'Where are the rest of the men?' I inquired.

" 'Locked up,' said the guard.

" 'And when do these get locked up?' I persisted.

" 'Oh,' he answered, 'at 11 or half-past...'

" 'When they get ready?' I suggested.

" 'Well, they're trusties,' he said. I found that a number of trusties were permitted to lock themselves up when they felt like retiring."

They were about to learn new ways under the new warden, but not until he himself had undergone a literal baptism of fire the next day, his first full day on the job.

Eighteen inmates whom he identified as drug addicts propped their mattresses against the cell doors and set fire to them as a protest. Their drug supplies had been cut off with nothing to ease withdrawal pangs.

The fires were extinguished "after a spectacular fight [followed by] a pandemonium of yells and banging on cell doors with iron buckets" which spread through the whole prison.

Groome made several unhappy discoveries in his first days as warden. First, Cherry Hill's location was bad. The city had grown up around it so that an escapee could quickly find cover in the home of a friend. There wasn't much anyone could do about that, but he helped in the planning of a successor institution out in the country at Graterford, Montgomery County.

Second, Eastern State was densely overcrowded, holding more than twice its prescribed number of inmates, and only three hundred of the then total of 1,600 were employed. Idleness was corroding the remainder.

Third, "the place crawled with dirt"—the source of its odor. He decided to begin with cleaning up.

The prisoners, he found were fed in their cells, and whatever they didn't eat they threw into the corridor where it remained until the following morning, attracting roaches and rats.

His first order was that all cells and corridors would be flushed and scrubbed at 7 a.m. each morning, then inspected. "You can't do it, wailed my old gentlemen, the guards. We haven't enough employees," Groome wrote.

"You have 1,300 idle men, and scrubbing a floor requires no special training, I pointed out."

He then called for each prisoner to bathe three times a week, instead of the prevailing once-a-week or less. Gradually, the prison's smell began to recede, and in a few months not a trace of it was reported.

Next, he turned to the contraband flowing into Cherry Hill. Liquor was plentiful, some of it from stills within the walls; ninety drug addicts most of the time were amply supplied with heroin, morphine or other narcotics; a search turned up half a dozen revolvers and 220 knives.

The sources of this stuff were visitors and guards. Patient internal detective work exposed guilty guards whom the warden fired.

Then he hired three State Police captains whom he appointed deputy wardens, and began turning over the guard force. Of the 110 guards, he ultimately discharged ninety-five for violation of rules, physical disability or for being unqualified to handle prisoners.

He replaced them—a reprise on how he manned the State Police—with "young, able-bodied men...with good past records, most of whom had 'excellent' discharges from the U.S. Army, Navy, Marine Corps or State Police."

Visitors, up to that point, could mingle freely with inmates while walking across the yard from the gate, allowing for drugs and liquor to be passed. A guard oversaw the visitor-prisoner encounter in the visiting cell. But "if the visitor would slip some of the guards a $5 bill," said Groome, "he could then give the inmate a package of drugs, a bottle of whiskey, a pistol or anything else..."

To correct the system, the warden set up a large visitors' room outside the penitentiary's second gate. Down its middle was a four-foot counter and above that a fine mesh wire screen to the ceiling. Visitors came to the room from the main gate, inmates to its other half, escorted from their cells. These measures stopped the contraband flow.

Three weeks after the new warden took office, six convicts, three of them armed with revolvers, in daylight one morning held up unarmed guards, climbed a ladder and escaped over the wall.

One was killed in New York; another arrested there and a third in Hawaii. A year later, the remaining three were still at large. Groome, stung by the breakout, fired six guards whose negligence allowed for the escape (he had not yet turned over the staff).

That was not the only escape of his first year. In November, Francis "Porky" Flynn and three other convicts escaped with the help of eighteen dollars given to Flynn by an inmate named James J. Fraley.

This infuriated the second deputy warden, Charles Santee, who beat Fraley, breaking his jaw and arm. Santee, one of Groome's State Police recruits, was later convicted of the assault and fired. At the time, the warden was on a trip to Europe.

After the first escape he ordered the ground-level guardhouses at each corner of the grounds hoisted to the top of the wall and armed the guards in them with repeater rifles and submachine guns.

Also needed, he believed, was a convict uniform that could be identified outside the prison as such. Stripes had earlier been replaced by plain blue denim in which an escapee could melt into the populace. Groome added to the uniform a distinguishing dark blue vertical strip.

*

The new warden decried "theorists" and reformers as "milksops." He blamed such for the reign of the tyrannical Four Horsemen, brought to power partly by a scheme of inmate democratic self-government.

Yet Groome was himself a reformer, at least in some aspects of penitentiary life. Food and dining, for example.

The 1923 grand jury had heard complaints that the food was not only bad but "there were animals and all sorts of things in it." Groome's clean-up order took care of the foreign matter and creatures.

Then he turned to menus. When he became warden, prisoners were fed the same meals day after day. The midday dinner, for example, was fried beef, potatoes and cabbage or turnips and black coffee, day in, day out.

He told the head cook who, by coincidence, came from Reval in Estonia, to make out a menu on Friday for the following week with meals varied each day.

"I allowed him, for instance to have the same breakfast Monday and Friday or the same dinner Tuesday and Saturday but there must be no day of repetition," he said. Menus were to be submitted first to the resident physician to be checked for adequate nourishment, then to the warden.

He gave some examples: breakfast, boiled rice and raisins or cereal with stewed prunes, coffee with milk and sugar. For midday dinner, roast ham or beef stew with onions, or fried country scrapple or fresh fish or a roast loin of beef or pork hocks with mashed potatoes and sauerkraut or lima beans, carrots and potatoes, or stewed tomatoes, spinach and canned corn, and always bread. Similar varieties for supper.

Equally important, he ended the century-long practice of in-cell feeding. He ripped out the cell yards in Blocks 4 and 5 and built two kitchens and mess halls, each seating eight hundred prisoners.

Long-time staffers predicted that collective dining would spawn riots. Since inmates already could talk in exercise yards—an innovation begun in 1913—Groome felt the objection didn't amount to much.

"I gave warning that eating in the mess hall was a privilege which, if abused, would be promptly withdrawn," he wrote. The only resulting "riots" in his five-year tenure were a prisoner throwing a bowl of soup on a guard and a fistfight between two inmates.

9

Slings, Arrows, Vindication

John Groome had been warden for almost a year when a Philadelphia grand jury in May 1924 inspected the prison and issued a critical report.

The jury recommended that he spend more time at the penitentiary and give its administration more personal attention. The jurors called for the removal of Deputy Warden Herbert Smith who, they said, ruled by "brutality and intimidation."

Smith had been accused by an earlier grand jury of placing an inmate so close to an open fire that the heat reportedly blistered him.

Prison conditions, the 1924 jurors reported, were "barbarous," and certain punishments "tend to degrade and terrorize the convicts and brutalize the officials and employees."

Groome did not suffer the criticism gladly. The recommendations, he said, were "not worth considering." Smith, he added, administers his office "with firm and impartial discipline founded on justice."

Out of 1,354 inmates, he said, the grand jury questioned only six, and those six were in punishment. Such a prisoner "will say anything to discredit the prison administration."

"As to performing my official duties in the prison instead of delegating them to subordinates," he said, "I consider I am better qualified by training and experience to decide how…administering the affairs of this institution shall be apportioned among my assistants, the ninety-four guards and numerous other employees, than a heterogeneous body of citizens drawn by lot and known as 'the grand jury,' the majority of whom never had any executive or administrative experience and never have seen the inside of a penitentiary, except possibly as inmates."

Not surprisingly, the grand jury was reported "incensed" at the warden's response. Myra Kennedy, a juror, told reporters that Smith actually ran the prison. "Colonel Groome," she added, "only collects the salary"—($7,500). She talked to fifty-one inmates, not six, she said.

The warden's final word: "There is no more truth in their report than in a fairy tale."

The jury's comments about punishments referred to what inmates called "the Klondike," a row of six cells in the upper tier of Cellblock 4, devoid of furniture and with walls painted black.

Klondike prisoners, given bread and water, were in solitary confinement, stripped of shoes and coats and equipped only with mattresses and blankets. Otherwise, Groome pointed out, the cells were like the prison's other seven hundred units, with toilet, ventilation, steam heat and enough daylight coming through the overhead ventilator "for reading of fine print." When the ventilator was closed to keep out the rain, however, all light in the cell was extinguished.

"Possibly they did not know," he added, "that confining men in these cells is not only the only form of punishment we have in this institution but is the mildest form of punishment...in any penal institution in the country."

Finally, Governor Pinchot had enough. The scion of a wealthy family and an adamant foe within the party of the state's Republican machine, he was an activist and an idealist—"the forester who beat the organization," in the words of the Philadelphia *Public Ledger*.

He had appointed Dr. Ellen C. Potter as Pennsylvania's first woman cabinet member, secretary of welfare, the department responsible for the penitentiary. He named her and three other officials, including two physicians, to thoroughly investigate ESP.

The governor's move prompted an about-face by Groome on the grand jury report. "I agree with [Pinchot] that the recommendations of a grand jury should not be ignored," he said.

The Potter Committee held hearings over four days at the penitentiary and heard testimony under oath from 139 prisoners. The committee's ten-thousand-word report was unanimous. It amounted to a complete vindication of Groome and his stewardship at Cherry Hill.

"He had the courage to undertake an almost impossible task when [the prison] was at its chaotic worst, and has in twelve months made an institution which was a disgrace to Pennsylvania a place of order, cleanliness and reasonable safety," the committee wrote.

"Moreover," they added, "we do not consider the criticisms made of Colonel Groome justified by the facts…. The Warden spends a very large part of his waking hours in the institution or in pursuit of its business outside the prison. He is absolutely familiar with all matters of policy and detail of method…excepting such detail as must by any executive be delegated to his subordinates."

The report noted that all but thirty of the inmates were engaged in some useful employment. On that point, Pinchot commented, "Warden Groome has performed a miracle in providing work for so many men…"

The Potter Committee heard frequent testimony, members wrote, that the prison's food was better than that provided to the U.S. Army in World War I.

They also found that garbage on the floor, rats, vermin and institution odor had been eliminated, as had the availability of narcotic drugs and alcohol.

They recommended that the Klondike cells be kept, seeing nothing in their use that was unduly cruel to inmates. The prison's more usual, and lesser, punishment consisted of withdrawing privileges, they observed.

"Persons confined in seclusion," they wrote, "should be under daily observation by the physician, which we are informed is the case."

As for the charge that Deputy Warden Smith placed an inmate so close to an open fire that he was blistered, the committee dismissed the allegation. The panel's two doctors examined the inmate and found no sign or scars of blisters. They accepted Smith's claim that he was merely helping the prisoner dry some wet clothing.

The plumbing, the committee reported, had been entirely renovated and is now "literally modern."

On the charge that inmates are "in a state of terror and are [filled] with a hatred of all authority...it is our conclusion, based on careful observation and inquiry, that this is not so," the committee wrote.

A large group of responsible prisoners, they added, testified that they are getting a "square deal," that Deputy Warden Smith is "a man of his word" and that everyone has a chance to be heard.

"There is today a sense of security and fair play...the morale of the institution is good."

Pinchot, receiving the report, expressed pride at the "remarkable progress made by Colonel Groome and the trustees." ESP, he said, had been a "sinkhole of iniquity," rife with drugs and graft, idle inmates and bad food.

The Potter investigation, he said, "clearly establishes two things: First, that the right spirit exists in the management of the institution and, second, that unusual progress has been made in carrying this spirit into effect."

The report, he added, "dispos[es] completely of the charges it deals with...." He pledged to Groome and the trustees "every support in my power to carry out the recommendations..."

Besides reading the report, Pinchot toured the old prison with Groome, the lean, six-foot-two governor towering five inches over the warden in his brass-buttoned uniform with three rows of military campaign and decoration ribbons above its left pocket.

After the tour the governor said he was especially impressed to learn that more than 90 percent of the inmates had gained weight since entering the institution. "Men who are treated brutally do not thrive on it," he said.

*

Groome, on his own, tried to dispel some rumors. Talking to a reporter later about his presence at the prison, said he worked there from 9 or 9:15 a.m. to 7 or 8 p.m. and had little time for recreation.

"Inferences have been made that I play golf every day, but this is not true, except that every morning at 6 o'clock I take about a hundred golf balls onto the polo field at [Haverford] and knock them off a tee."

(The Groomes were golfers. John's brother, Harry, is credited with introducing the game to the Philadelphia area. As resident secretary of the Philadelphia Country Club, his duty was to offer "suitable sports" to the members.

(One autumn Sunday in 1891, he and colleagues took three cans that had held French peas and sank them in the club's lawn in a triangle, about seventy-five yards on a side. Swinging imported clubs, rented at twenty-five cents per half hour, they knocked balls from can to can. "The thing was regarded as a huge joke," Harry Groome said later.)

Cherry Hill's cellblock of fifty women had long bothered John Groome. "...there could be no peace in the prison, nor any real order, nor much approach to decency as long as a cell bock remained occupied by women," he wrote in the *Post*.

A new state law allowed for transfer of inmates from overcrowded prisons by court order. The warden quickly won court approval of sending all the women prisoners to jails in the counties where they had been arrested.

The only other group noisome to Groome was "degenerate" men, likely a reference to homosexual acts. These inmates he segregated.

The idleness of 1,300 prisoners was a major challenge for him. He filled two hours of each good day with outdoor recreation. Two corners of the grounds he got paved and made into four handball courts. A basketball court of sorts was created; baseball and football were played in season. Boxing matches were held between men of similar size.

He learned of a forty-five-piece brass band in the prison, an orchestra of eighteen players and a string band of twenty-five. Up to then, they played only on holidays. Groome got the brass band to play every day for an hour and a half, beginning at 6 p.m. when prisoners were locked into their cells.

"This made locking them up a less dreary business [and gave] the inmates something to think about and anticipate," he said. He scheduled the orchestra and string band to play four or five times a week.

The performers ended up winning considerable celebrity. Directed by a volunteer musician, Albert Hoxie, they played seven concerts in 1924 and '25 broadcast by radio station WIP. The performances drew "thousands" of complimentary telegrams and letters, Groome wrote in his annual report to the prison trustees.

The three hundred employed inmates worked in Department of Welfare shops, including automobile repair, printing and shoe repair. State law forbade prisoners from making or selling articles except through the department.

But Groome was determined to fight idleness. He learned about the making of rag carpets, imported rags into the prison and acquired one hundred sewing machines, thus employing a hundred carpet makers, he wrote in his *Post* article.

"People who are afraid prison labor might cut down their own wages...said our rag industry was against the law and threatened to have me arrested," the warden reported. Since the carpets were not being sold on the open market, however, he ignored the threat.

A Philadelphia friend, Henry Brock, did set up an outlet shop in center-city, where penitentiary-made articles could be sold "without infringing the law," said Groome.

Ultimately, a great variety of articles came into the shop. He heard about a North Carolina caned chair company that needed workers: they sent chair frames to the prison where twenty-five inmates caned them for sale.

Through inquiries, the warden identified among inmates iron workers who were set to making weather vanes, fireplace fenders, etc., tinsmiths who made waste baskets bearing painted designs, wood workers who made boxes, ship models and the like. All the money from sales went to the prison workers.

Late in Groome's five-year wardenship, up to nine hundred inmates began working on the construction of the new prison at Graterford.

By 1925 he could report that 1,265 of the 1,386 ESP population—91 percent—were working, although 509 of them were uncompensated. Still, they were no longer idle.

The penitentiary's trustees were impressed. "The Board again wishes to commend the administration of the prison...under Colonel John C. Groome, warden, and his deputies," wrote Fleisher in 1925.

"The improvement in the morale of prisoners, noted in last year's report, has continued, and the physical condition of the penitentiary has been kept up to a high standard in the face of seemingly insurmountable handicaps resulting from the inadequacy of the present century-old plant."

The warden himself made a similar observation. "When I first became warden," he wrote, "the prisoners used to pass me with an ugly, hangdog scowl. Before I resigned...there were few who did not look me in the eye with a pleasant 'good morning.' "

He said he was told later by an ex-inmate that among themselves prisoners called him "the Czar, but the 'good morning' was not compulsory."

He also secured a pay raise for the guards. One reason that earlier guards had been grafters, he said, was that they could not live on their pay. And he gave them new uniforms that he had designed. Guards who previously had napped or smoked on duty responded favorably to discipline, he claimed.

Ever the military man, Groome got the guards to salute their superiors and by the time he left "nine out of ten prisoners either would salute or remove their hats when you met them, and they did it voluntarily."

The trustees, he wrote, had predicted that it would be impossible to sign on competent guards at Cherry Hill. "When I resigned," he noted, "there were forty-seven more applications than we could fill."

Groome resigned his post effective February 15, 1928, a little shy of five years on the job. He could look back with satisfaction on changes for the good he had brought to the old prison.

Physically, the plant had been cleaned and spruced up; it was free of drugs and alcohol; guards were disciplined, better paid and newly uniformed. The great majority of inmates were employed, they were far better fed and dining together and their recreation much improved.

The trustees accepted his resignation with regret. "It was largely through Colonel Groome's efforts that the high standard of the Institution was obtained, and the Board feels it has lost a valuable and efficient administrator," wrote Fleisher in May 1928.

Groome gave no reason for leaving. But he had been in some kind of public service for forty-six years and, as he approached his sixty-sixth birthday in March, he was beginning to suffer from arthritis.

The antiquated, cramped Eastern State Penitentiary continued operations until 1970, housing such notorious convicts as Al Capone and Willie Sutton. Five years before that it had been designated a National Historic Landmark. Except in winter months, visitors tour it daily.

10

Boca Raton, Final Years

As he stepped out the warden's office at the Eastern Pen, an *Evening Bulletin* reporter asked Groome what was next for him.

He said he was going to be the vice president of something called the Spanish River Land Company.

Its business was land development in Boca Raton, Florida, thirty miles south of Palm Beach, but its headquarters was in Philadelphia. The company's president was Clarence H. Geist, a utilities multi-millionaire with a palatial home in the Philadelphia suburb Villanova.

Groome and Geist knew each other; they moved in the same social circle. It is likely that perceived mutual benefits prompted the vice presidency offer.

Membership in the Spanish River company was limited to "persons distinguished in public service, the learned professions or in business..." What better way to attract such members than to have in the vice president's chair the eminent former head of the Pennsylvania State Police and warden of the Eastern State Penitentiary?

For Groome the position would have looked simply like an opportunity to make some easy money.

The first permanent settlement at Boca Raton (the name derives from the Spanish *Boca de Ratones*, Mouth of the Sharp-Pointed Rocks) was in 1875. The town was not incorporated until 1925. The Spanish River, now subterranean, ran through it.

At stake for the Spanish River Company were the holdings of the bankrupt Mizner Development Corporation—fifteen thousand acres of coastal land at Boca Raton and the 150-room Cloister Inn.

Geist, a self-made man off an Indiana farm, controlled more than one hundred gas, electric and water utilities in eleven states. He bought the Mizner package, worth $40 million on paper, for $7 million and turned it into the Boca Raton Club. The inn, to which Geist added three hundred rooms, became the clubhouse.

He set up a syndicate, shares of which subscribers could purchase at $5,000 to $20,000, giving them club membership and property rights. Subscribers included Philadelphia notables with names like Cassatt, Glendenning, Newbold, Lloyd, Gates and Hopkinson.

Nowhere in the papers or history of Boca Raton does Groome's name appear.

In his history of the State Police, Conti says ill health cut short Groome's association with the Boca Raton project. His health, however, did not prevent his accepting one last public post—Governor John S. Fisher's appointment to the board of trustees of Eastern State Penitentiary.

Groome's health began to spiral downwards in 1930. It even became something of a public issue.

On July 26 of that year the *Evening Bulletin* ran a five-inch story headlined "Col. Groome Better." Stating that he had been bedridden for several weeks "with physicians in daily attendance," the article said he was improved but didn't disclose what the health problem was.

He suffered severe arthritis, but what killed him, according to his death certificate, was primarily prostate cancer with the contributing cause of metastases "in all bones of the body."

He died Sunday morning, August 31, 1930, at age sixty-eight in his Haverford home. Flags at all Pennsylvania State Police posts were ordered flown at half-staff for thirty days and all personnel of the force were told to wear a black crepe band four inches wide on the left sleeve halfway between elbow and shoulder.

The funeral was held at noon three days later at the family's church, St. Peter's Episcopal, at Third and Pine Streets. It is one of Philadelphia's most historic churches, dating to 1761.

A *Philadelphia Inquirer* article the day before the funeral named the eight active pallbearers, leaders of four organizations Groome had served. It added:

"At Colonel Groome's own request, no military display will mark the services." Were his wishes disregarded? Here is the account of the service in the First City Troop annals.

"The funeral of honorary Captain Groome was attended in full-dress uniform on September 3 at St. Peter's Church. The Troop headed the procession into the Church...followed by a detachment of the Pennsylvania State Police, officers of the 305th Cavalry, officers of the 79th Division, representatives of the Eastern Penitentiary and honorary rolls [of the Troop] in civilian dress led by Honorary Captain Thomas Cadwalader."

He was buried in Laurel Hill Cemetery in Philadelphia.

His estate was reported to total $234,599, only a fraction of the wealth of, say, his friend Geist. But Groome had spent his life in public service where money doesn't usually pile up. Nonetheless, in 1930 dollars the estate was a tidy sum.

He willed it to his wife, Agnes, and their three children, John Jr., Mrs. Agnes R. Dixon and Mrs. Martha G. Thompson. The children quitclaimed their shares in favor of their mother.

Presumably, those shares came back to them when Agnes died seven years later at age sixty-nine. She was esteemed in the Groome family for her hospitality in making her home available for those who needed it.

What are we to make of the life of John C. Groome? "Groome devoted a lifetime to public service," Lt. Col. Conti, the historian, wrote. "He was indeed a great man."

He was born into a family of privilege and some wealth. He could have kept going down that road with the Kendrick firm or even as a wine wholesaler.

He chose instead to serve the public. He did not always reach out eagerly at first for those opportunities. Sometimes he rejected them initially but then, whether from pressure by others or his own conscience, he seized the challenge and gave it everything he had.

The results, certainly in the major endeavors of his life, were impressive. He organized and administered the Pennsylvania State Police so well that it became a national model—first and best.

At Eastern State Penitentiary he may not have broken new ground nationally in prison operation, but he surely broke worn out patterns there and put the antique facility on the road to maximum and humane serviceability.

In Europe he confronted a daunting combination of tests. He ended up meeting them and in the process saving the lives of thousands upon thousands of children and adults.

All the while he even managed to have some fun, as with those hundreds of golf balls he smacked off the tee with his hickory-shafted clubs on the polo field across from his home.

Bibliography

Anderson, David M. and David Killingray, eds. *Policing the Empire.* Manchester, U.K. and New York: Manchester University Press, 1991.

Conti, Lt. Col. Philip M. (ret.) *The Pennsylvania State Police, A History of Service to the Commonwealth, 1905 to the Present.* Harrisburg: Stackpole Books, 1977.

Cornell, Robert J. *The Anthracite Coal Strike of 1902.* New York: Russell and Russell, 1971.

Curl, Donald W. and John P. Johnson. *Boca Raton, A Pictorial History.* Virginia Beach: Donning Company, 1990.

Dulles, Foster Rhea. *Labor in America, a History.* New York: Thomas Y. Crowell, 1966.

Finegan, James W. *A Centennial Tribute to Golf in Philadelphia.* Philadelphia: The Golf Association of Philadelphia, 1996.

Groome, John C. "The Riot Call." *Saturday Evening Post.* Jan. 25, 1930.

Harbord, James G. *The American Army in France, 1917-1919.* Boston: Little Brown & Co., 1936.

Hoover, Herbert C. *The Memoirs of Herbert Hoover: The Years of Adventure, 1874-1920.* New York: The Macmillan Co., 1951.

Jackson, Stanley. *J. P. Morgan.* Briarcliff Manor, N.Y.: Stein and Day, 1983.

Johnston, Norman. *Eastern State Penitentiary: Crucible of Good Intentions.* Philadelphia: Philadelphia Museum of Art, 1994.

Johnston, Norman. *Escapes from Eastern State Penitentiary*. Philadelphia: Eastern State Penitentiary Historic Site, undated.

Mayo, Katherine. *Justice to All: The Story of the Pennsylvania State Police*. Boston: Houghton Mifflin Co., 1917.

Miller, Char. *Gifford Pinchot and the Making of Modern Environmentalism*. Washington, D.C.: Island Press, 2001.

Palmer, Stanley H. *Police and Protest in England and Ireland, 1780-1850*. Cambridge: Cambridge University Press, 1988.

Peare, Catherine Owens. *The Herbert Hoover Story*. New York: Thomas Y. Crowell Co., 1928.

Pennypacker, Samuel W. *The Autobiography of a Pennsylvanian*. Philadelphia: John C. Winston Co., 1918.

Smith, Bruce. *The State Police: Organization and Administration*. New York: The Macmillan Company, 1925.

Stevens, Sylvester K. *Pennsylvania: Birthplace of a Nation*. New York: Random House, 1964.

Surface, Frank M. and Raymond L. Bland. *American Food in the World War and Reconstruction Period*. Stanford, CA: Stanford University Press, 1931.

Weigley, Russell F., ed. *Philadelphia: A 300-Year History*. New York: W. W. Norton & Co., 1982.

Annals of the First Troop Philadelphia City Cavalry, 1774-1914. undated.

History of the First Troop Philadelphia City Cavalry, 1914-1948. undated.

Annual Reports, Eastern State Penitentiary, 1923-1928.

Annual Reports, Pennsylvania State Police, 1906-1917.

The Anthracite Coal Strike Commission. *Report to the President on the Anthracite Coal Strike of May-October, 1902*. 1903.

Organization of American Relief in Europe, 1918-1919. Stanford, CA: Stanford University Press, 1943.

The Spanish River Papers. Boca Raton: Boca Raton Historical Society, 1987-1988.

Index

About the Author

After graduating from Yale in 1943, Harry Toland spent three years in the Marine Corps in World War II and then began a forty-two-year career in journalism. More than thirty-one of those years were at the *Evening Bulletin* in Philadelphia as labor reporter, regional columnist, deputy metropolitan editor and editorial writer/columnist.

Before retirement, he was for two years associate editor of *The Episcopalian*, then the Episcopal Church's national journal. The author of three other books, Toland lives in Wallingford, Pennsylvania, with his wife, Sibby.

1270572

Made in the USA